# THE WORLD OF THE
# HUMMINGBIRD

# THE WORLD OF THE
# HUMMINGBIRD

## HARRY THURSTON

Sierra Club Books
San Francisco

PAGES II–III

*A white-necked jacobin of*

*Costa Rica.*

TOM J. ULRICH


PAGE IV

*A cinnamon hummingbird,*

*native to the Pacific slopes of*

*Mexico and the Yucatán*

*Peninsula.*

KEVIN SCHAFER

http://www.sierraclub.org/books

Originally published in Canada by Greystone Books, a division of Douglas & McIntyre Ltd, 2323 Quebec Street, Suite 201, Vancouver, B.C. V5T 4S7.

LIBRARY OF CONGRESS CATALOGING-IN-PUBLICATION DATA

Thurston, Harry
    (Nature of hummingbirds)
    The world of the hummingbird/Harry Thurston.
        p.   cm.
    Includes bibliographical references.
    ISBN 1-57805-043-X
    1. Hummingbirds  2. Hummingbirds—Pictorial works  I. Title
QL696.A558T48 1999              598.7'64–dc21              99-14097

Editing by Nancy Flight
Jacket and text design by Gabi Proctor/DesignGeist
Front jacket photograph by Wendy Shattil/Bob Rozinski
Back jacket photograph by Kevin Schafer
Printed and bound in Hong Kong by C&C Offset Printing Co., Ltd

10 9 8 7 6 5 4 3 2 1

# CONTENTS

# ACKNOWLEDGMENTS

*Where is the person who, on seeing this lovely fragment of the rainbow moving on humming winglets through the air, suspended in it as if by magic, and flitting from one flower to another, would not pause and turn his mind toward the Almighty Creator?*

— JOHN JAMES AUDUBON, *The Birds of America* (1840–44)

I am grateful to biologist/naturalist Sheri Williamson of the Southeastern Arizona Bird Observatory in Bisbee, Arizona, for reviewing the manuscript and making many useful suggestions. The responsibility for any errors is wholly my own, however. I am also grateful to Ted Eubanks of Texas for answering my questions regarding the migration of ruby-throated hummingbirds; to William A. Calder, Department of Ecology and Evolutionary Biology, University of Arizona, Tucson, Arizona, for sharing his expertise; and to Gail and Philip Mosley, my northern neighbors with whom I share special delight in our little tropical visitors. I thank Kathy Hubenschmidt of the Arizona State Museum for finding the photograph of the Apache war shield from Western Apache Material Culture, the Goodwin and Guenther Collections. I also thank my editor, Nancy Flight, and the general editor of the series, Candace Savage, for their always gentle and steady guidance.

*In memory of Charlotte Warwick Thurston, who so brightened our lives*

FACING PAGE

*In an impressive show of aerial acrobatics, a broad-billed hummingbird dips its wings and fans its tail.* WAYNE & HELEN LANKINEN

# INTRODUCTION

To have hummingbirds buzzing about my backyard is a wish that I share with the millions of other North Americans who, like me, station feeders or plant hummingbird gardens to attract them. My life is brightened by the flashy appearance of these feathered jewels, out of all proportion to their size.

There is a freshness to every encounter with a hummingbird, as if it had a unique power to appeal to childlike perception. The special qualities of this group seem to revive and sustain our fascination with, and faith in, the creative powers of Nature. As the nineteenth-century British ornithologist John Gould observed: ". . . the pleasure which I experience on seeing a Humming Bird is as great at the present moment as when first I saw one. During the first 20 years of my acquaintance with these wonderful works of creation my thoughts were often directed to them in the day, and my night dreams have not unfrequently carried me to their native forests in the distant country of America."

Hummingbirds in all their glittering diversity have long held a special place in the cosmology of Native peoples throughout North and South America. To the Taíno indigenous people of the Caribbean and Florida, the first people to meet Columbus, the hummingbird is "the spreader of life on the Earth." They believed that the hummingbird first carried tobacco to their people. Because tobacco was considered a medicinal plant, hummingbirds became known as "doctor birds," a generic name that still applies today in the West Indies to several species, including the streamertail. This green-and-black hummingbird sports two 15- to 15.5-centimeter-long (6- to 7-inch-long) tail feathers—"streamers"—which make a humming sound in flight. This most spectacular of hummingbirds, *Trochilus polytmus*, is, as ornithologist Alexander F. Skutch has noted, the "name-bearer of the whole hummingbird family," the Trochilidae.

The Cherokee also have a story about hummingbirds and tobacco. "In the beginning of the world, when people and animals were all the same," so the story

FACING PAGE

*Using its needlelike bill, a ruby-throated hummingbird injects food into the gaping mouth of a hungry nestling.*
ROGER ERIKSSON

XI

goes, the sole tobacco plant was stolen by the geese, Dragûl'Kû, and carried away. Many animals tried to retrieve the plant, for the people were suffering without it. But all were killed trying. Finally, Hummingbird offered to try. Because he was so small and so swift, he made off with the plant before the geese knew what had happened.

The boldness of the hummingbird clan also accounts for its important role in Aztec religion. The most powerful of the Aztec gods was Huitzilopochtli, whose name comes from a compound word derived from *huitzilin*, meaning "hummingbird" and "sorcerer that spits fire." The hummingbird played a central role in the genesis story of Huitzilopochtli, who was conceived from a ball of hummingbird feathers that fell from the sky, impregnating the goddess Coatlicue. Huitzilopochtli himself was depicted wearing the head of a hummingbird as a helmet, and Aztec royalty and priests often wore capes adorned with hummingbird feathers. In addition, Aztec warriors were thought to be reincarnated as hummingbirds, probably because of the birds' fierce territoriality.

Perhaps even more fundamental to the agrarian Aztecs was their belief that hummingbirds represented the seasons of spring and summer. When the hummingbirds (which were thought to hibernate) returned in spring, they brought with them the rain and thus the rebirth of life itself.

The belief that hummingbirds brought rain also took root among the pueblo peoples of the arid American Southwest. The Tohono O'Odham of the Sonoran Desert, which stretches from northern Mexico into southern Arizona, say that the hummingbird saved them from drought and starvation by finding the wind and the rain. The Hopi, who occupy desert lands north of the Tohono O'Odham, fashion sacred hummingbird *kachinas* to honor Tocha, "the bringer of rain."

The significance of hummingbirds to New World peoples has persisted in Mexican folklore, which often depicts hummingbirds holding up the baby Jesus'

diapers. This iconography arose, it is thought, when the Spanish, in an effort to convert Native Americans to Christianity, adopted the return of the migratory hummingbirds as a symbol of the Resurrection.

Hummingbirds also made a profound impression on the European mind. Perhaps none of the early naturalists expressed the wonder at this newfound family of birds more cogently than John Lawson, who, in 1709, wrote in *A New Voyage to Carolina:* "The humming-bird is the miracle of all our winged animals."

John James Audubon observed: "The Hummingbird does not shun mankind as much as other birds generally do." This apparent lack of concern about humans has always endeared the bold little birds to us. Not only do hummingbirds seem to tolerate humans generally, but they seem to possess some personal knowledge of us as individuals—or at least some memory of a specific place and time, and of our presence in that specific context. Among hummingbird lovers, there is much anecdotal evidence attesting to the fact that hummingbirds possess an excellent memory and even form individual, long-term bonds with humans.

The hummingbird chattering at my study window, imploring me to hang my feeder promptly, I'm sure, is the same individual who buzzed about my deck, supping from my feeder last summer. When I go out to investigate, he reappears, stalling only a foot in front of my face. He shuttles back and forth, chattering loudly, before making a beeline to the empty space where the feeder should be hung. He hovers there, as if making an accusatory pause in our visual communication. The message is clear, as is the demonstration that this hummingbird possesses a memory of where the feeder was and my role in replenishing it.

Such a relationship with a wild creature is rare. When the creature is as colorful and dynamic as a hummingbird, the sense of privilege and responsibility is deeply felt.

FACING PAGE

*At 6.5 grams, nearly twice the weight of a ruby-throat, the black-throated mango of Costa Rica is one of the larger species of hummingbirds.*

BARRETT & MACKAY PHOTO

# FEATHERED JEWELS

*Part One*

# AND FLOWER KISSERS

*No sooner has the spring sun restored the vernal season, and caused millions of plants to open their leaves and blossoms to his genial beams, than the little Hummingbird is seen.*

— JOHN JAMES AUDUBON, *The Birds of America* (1840–44)

Of the seasonal round of events in the naturalist's year, none quite delights me so much as the sudden appearance of the first ruby-throated hummingbird of spring. This aeronautic marvel hovers at my study window, then shoots off like a pebble launched from a slingshot. Everything about this Tom Thumb of the avian world is improbable: its size, or lack of; its fluorescence, the namesake gorget carving the light into jewel-like flakes; the hum of its wings, a blur of matter more audible than visible.

It is impossible to mistake hummingbirds for any other species, not only because of their hovering flight, but also because of their appearance. Their diminutive size is closer to that of insects than to that of other birds, a fact that gave rise to the obsolete sobriquet "bee birds." To many, their most distinctive trait is their brilliant coloring, which John James Audubon compared to the "glittering garment of the rainbow." The beguiling hues of hummingbirds, and the unusual phenomenon of color change as they rotate in space like tiny satellites, have inspired a plethora of epithets evocative of color, movement, and light: "winged gems," "feathered

FACING PAGE

*A ruby-throated hummingbird feeds from pendant flowers hanging from flexible stalks. The hovering ability of hummingbirds is critical to exploiting such difficult-to-reach food sources.*

WAYNE & HELEN LANKINEN

THE ANGLE AT WHICH

THE LIGHT STRIKES

THE HUMMINGBIRD'S

SCALE-LIKE FEATHERS

IS THE DIFFERENCE

BETWEEN THE COLORS

BEING DAZZLINGLY

VISIBLE OR ENTIRELY

OBSCURED.

jewels," and "rainbow atoms," and such South American common names as "rays of the sun" and "tresses of the day star."

Even casual hummingbird observers have noticed that as hummingbirds hover, they flash their dazzling, iridescent colors one moment, then appear dark and dull the next—like a lighthouse flashing and occulting its signal. The phenomenon of interference accounts for this now-you-see-it, now-you-don't light show. The angle at which the light strikes the hummingbird's scale-like feathers is the difference between the colors being dazzlingly visible or entirely obscured. We observe a similar rainbow effect when we look at a soap bubble or thin layer of oil on water.

As with many birds, the most colorful of the pair is the male. The male's throat patch, or gorget, reflects the full spectrum of color in different species—ruby, magenta, green, blue, and violet.

Flashing the tiny beacon of his namesake ruby throat, my springtime male darts away and returns as if on a miniature monorail, squeaking a complaint that I imagine goes something like this: "I'm back, so why haven't you hung the feeder yet?"

It is May 20, 1997, in Nova Scotia, near the northern limit of the ruby-throated hummingbird's breeding territory. To my surprise, a check of a half century's ornithological records reveals that May 20 is the average date for the ruby-throat's arrival in these northern climes. So, indeed, I must consider myself tardy in welcoming this Neotropical migrant to its summer home.

More than a century before, on May 17, 1856—not far south of here—Henry David Thoreau welcomed "a splendid male hummingbird" to his Maine woods: "Its hum was heard afar at first, like that of a large bee, bringing a larger summer. This sight and sound would make me think I was in the tropics—in Demerara or Maracaibo."

FACING PAGE

*A male ruby-throated hummingbird displays its namesake gorget, scalelike feathers under the chin which refract light to produce iridescent effects.*

JAMES H. ROBINSON

A northerner like Thoreau, I too have always been struck by the hummingbird's exoticism, as if the bird itself was a bright bit of the tropics, spalled off and spun north. In reality, this tropical illusion reflects the present-day distribution of this far-flung family and its evolution through time.

## A TROPICAL FAMILY

Hummingbirds are concentrated near the equator, with diversity declining the farther north or south one goes. Not surprisingly, Ecuador hosts the most species. Once, on a brief stopover in Quito, I watched a hummingbird working the purple blossoms of a flowering vine trailing along a stone wall on a downtown street, though, I confess, I have no idea which of the 150 Ecuadorean species the bird might have been.

Hummingbirds are restricted to the New World. With approximately 320 recognized species, they are the second-largest family of birds in the Western Hemisphere, outnumbered only by American flycatchers. Hummingbirds are most closely related to the swifts, fast-flying, non-perching birds that feed exclusively on insects, and have traditionally been grouped with them in the order Apodiformes.

They breed from Alaska (the rufous hummingbird) to Tierra del Fuego (the Chilean firestar) and include the smallest bird in the world, the 6.25-centimeter (2.5-inch) bee hummingbird, native to Cuba, as well as the relatively colossal—for a hummingbird—21.25-centimeter (8.5-inch) Patagonia giant.

Mexico is the richest hummingbird haven in North America, boasting some fifty species. Twenty-three species have been reported in the United States and Canada. Some of these sightings are of species that have wandered far from home, such as the rare Xantu's hummingbird native to Baja California that showed up in Gibsons, British Columbia, in November 1997. Only sixteen species have been known to nest in North America, and of these, only eleven commonly breed north

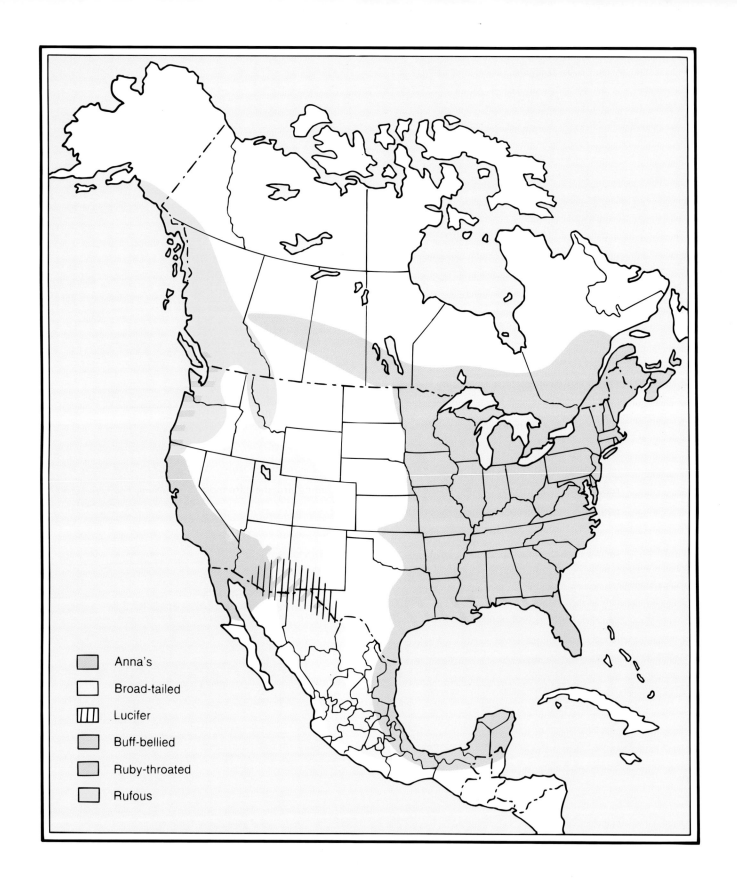

Anna's

Broad-tailed

Lucifer

Buff-bellied

Ruby-throated

Rufous

of Mexico (Figure 1). In the United States several North American hummingbirds, including Allen's, blue-throated, broad-billed, and Costa's, have breeding ranges largely restricted to the Southwest, with Texas, Arizona, New Mexico, and California, respectively, boasting the most species. The breeding range of the broad-tailed hummingbird extends farther north, to include southeastern Oregon, Nevada, Utah, western Wyoming, and Colorado. Lucifer, magnificent, berylline, white-eared, and violet-crowned hummingbirds barely venture over the border from Mexico, seldom being observed outside such hummingbird hotspots as Arizona's southeastern mountains. The breeding range of the buff-bellied hummingbird hugs the Gulf coast of Texas, east to Louisiana. Five species of the North American hummingbirds do have a wide distribution: ruby-throated hummingbirds breed throughout the eastern half of North America, west almost to the Rockies in Canada; rufous hummingbirds are widespread in the Northwest, reaching as far north as Alaska; and the black-chinned hummingbird, the third most widely distributed species, breeds in the mountains from Mexico north to British Columbia. Anna's hummingbirds occupy the Pacific coast from Baja California to southern British Columbia. A high-mountain hummingbird, making its way northward into Canada is the calliope, the smallest North American breeding bird. Despite its diminutive size (it is about a third the size of the smallest warblers), it lives up to its heroic name, after the muse of epic poetry. Not only the smallest long-distance migratory bird in the world, it survives, despite its small size, in the chilling mountain terrain of northwestern North America.

Despite their apparent fragility, hummingbirds are hardy and highly adaptable. They occupy a wide variety of ecological habitats in western North America, including desert, arid woodland, mountain forests, and arid scrubland; in eastern North America, the distribution of the ruby-throat coincides with deciduous and mixed woodlands.

FIGURE 1

*Breeding ranges of six North American species demonstrate the diversity and wide distribution of habitats that hummingbirds exploit, from Alaska to Mexico. Several species, such as Anna's hummingbirds, are expanding their traditional ranges. The range for Lucifer hummingbirds extends from the Valley of Mexico in Distrito Federal (not shown) to the U.S. border.* ADAPTED FROM DAN TRUE, 1993, *HUMMINGBIRDS OF NORTH AMERICA: ATTRACTING, FEEDING, AND PHOTOGRAPHING* (ALBUQUERQUE: UNIVERSITY OF NEW MEXICO PRESS).

To a surprising degree, however, hummingbirds are mountain-country species—surprising because a warm-blooded animal as small as a hummingbird must wage a constant struggle to maintain its body temperature. The greatest species diversity occurs in the Andes and decreases, with altitude, in the eastern lowlands of South America. A similar pattern predominates in North America, where several species occupy the mountainous western regions of the continent, while the ruby-throated hummingbird is the only species common to the lowlands east of the Mississippi.

## AERIAL OARS: THE ORIGINS OF HUMMING FLIGHT

It appears that hummingbirds evolved in the tropics, where they are still most abundant, and radiated out to the ends of the Western Hemisphere. Their diversity and wide distribution tell us that the family is indeed ancient. But hummingbird bones are so small and fragile that there are no fossil remains to help scientists precisely piece together the evolutionary history of hummingbirds. Many believe, however, that hummingbirds and swifts evolved from a common ancestor. For this reason, in the past the two groups have been slotted into the same order, the Apodiformes.

Hummingbirds and swifts do share a number of anatomical and behavioral characteristics. Both lay long, white elliptical eggs. Also, some swifts build their nests on the underside of palm leaves, as do the hermit hummingbirds of the tropics, an uncharacteristically drab clan that is considered the most primitive of the hummingbirds.

Perhaps the most convincing similarity is that both groups are superb fliers. Their shared aerial abilities derive from a number of anatomical adaptations. Both types of birds have a shortened upper arm and forearm and greatly elongated hand

Facing page

*A long-tailed hermit belongs
to the most primitive and plain-
colored clan of hummingbirds,
the hermits.* PETE OXFORD/
BBC NATURAL HISTORY UNIT

bones; the hummingbird wing has been described as "all hand." As well, both species have an enlarged sternum with a deep keel for the attachment of robust flight muscles. (Hummingbirds also have two more pairs of ribs than most land birds, including swifts—eight rather than six—which protect them from the extraordinary stresses they are subjected to as they stop on a dime and accelerate to maximum speed in an instant.) Each group also has large forearm muscles, facilitating greater maneuverability in flight.

Despite these similarities, the two groups have some subtle but significant differences in wing anatomy, leading some researchers to believe that hummingbirds and swifts did not have a common ancestor but independently evolved similar flight mechanisms. This process of convergent evolution occurs when organisms with a different ancestry develop anatomical similarities as a result of adopting similar lifestyles—in this case, catching insects. It is believed that the first hummingbirds were entirely insectivorous, and today, the most primitive group of hummingbirds, the hermits, continues to be largely insect eaters.

Although insects still form a vital component of the hummingbird diet, most hummingbirds are primarily nectar eaters, and in order to take advantage of this food source, they must be able to hover. True hovering flight is a unique adaptation of hummingbirds, whereby they suspend themselves in the air, in a stationary position, without the aid of a wind or thermal updraft, and then instantly accelerate in any direction or even fly upside down for short distances.

This hovering flight is only possible because hummingbirds have extremely flexible shoulder joints. Their wings, which have been aptly described as "aerial oars," can move in all directions and rotate through nearly 180 degrees, allowing the greatest possible control over the direction of flight. Swifts' joints are more rigid, and so they are restricted to flapping their wings in an up-and-down motion as other birds do.

Not only the bone structure but also the musculature of hummingbirds accounts for their uncanny ability to maneuver in any direction and to accelerate and decelerate almost instantaneously. Hummingbirds have the largest breast muscles in relation to body size of any birds; these muscles account for 30 percent of body weight (in weak flyers, the same muscles constitute only 15 percent of a bird's weight). These massive "pecs" consist of two muscle bundles: the depressors, which power the downstroke; and the elevators, which control the recovery stroke. In most birds, the elevators have only 5 to 10 percent of the mass of the depressors and, being weak, function only to lift the wing. In hummingbirds, however, the two muscle groups are about equal in size. The large elevators convert the upstroke into a power stroke, providing both propulsion and lift.

As a hummingbird hovers, beating its wings backward and forward, the tips of the primary feathers on the hand portion of the wing describe a figure-eight pattern, with the "eight" lying on its side. On both the forward and backward strokes, the front edge of the wing leads, so that on the backstroke the wing is actually turned upside down. In effect, the forward and backward strokes, while providing both lift and propulsion, cancel each other out—and the bird can maintain its stationary position, an ability critical to its strategy of feeding on nectar. The wings operate like the rotors of a helicopter. By tilting the plane of the wing movement upward, the bird can move up or backward; by tilting the wing downward, it can hover forward. As the wings beat back and forth, at the rate of 20 to 80 times per second, they produce the namesake "humming" sound. During courtship dives, males may beat their wings as many as 200 times per second, by far the fastest rate of all birds.

Their unique hovering flight and the anatomical adaptations that have made it possible suggest that hummingbirds are birds of an entirely different feather.

*Facing page*

*Like aerial oars, the wings of a hovering Anna's hummingbird describe a figure-eight pattern, allowing the bird to maintain a stationary position.* Wayne & Helen Lankinen

*A ruby-throated hummingbird thrusts its bill into the corolla of a trumpet creeper flower. This system of trumpet-shaped flowers and long-billed pollinators — hummingbirds — has co-evolved to benefit both bird and plant.*

ADAM JONES

14

I MARVEL AT THE BIRD'S

FASTIDIOUS MANNER,

ITS PRECISION, AS IT

PROBES EACH OF THE

MINUSCULE NECTAR

RESERVOIRS,

ADJUSTING ITS

POSITION MILLIMETERS

AT A TIME, BLOSSOM

TO BLOSSOM.

Some researchers have recommended that hummingbirds be placed in their own order, the Trochiliformes, separate from the swifts, and that this order be placed at the very top of the nonpasserines (nonperching birds), indicating that it is the most highly evolved of all the nonpasserine orders.

## FLOWER KISSERS

Half a dozen hummingbirds exploit my feeder in the summer, making forays from the nearby apple tree or tending the feeder from the clothesline, where they cling by their tiny black feet like animated clothespins. This morning, I notice my feeder is again getting low, which is hardly surprising, because one of my home hummers feeds every two to three minutes, sometimes supping the contents thirty times before flying off, or frequently being driven off by a competitor. As I go out to replenish the sugar solution, I watch as one of my impatient visitors stalls in front of the flower basket hung by the screen door. The purplish-blue blossoms of the trailing *Lobelia* are tiny, barely large enough to accommodate the hummer's needlelike bill. I marvel at the bird's fastidious manner, its precision, as it probes each of the minuscule nectar reservoirs, adjusting its position millimeters at a time, blossom to blossom. It accomplishes this operation with such delicacy I can see why the Portuguese coined the term *beija flor*, or "flower kissers."

Just as human beings have evolved to make best use of their hands to procure food, ornithologist Alexander F. Skutch has pointed out that the whole form of a bird has evolved to make best use of its bill, whether it is designed to crack seeds, hawk insects, tear flesh, or sip nectar. In the case of hummingbirds, the long, slender bill is adapted for probing the tubular corollas—the whorl of outer petals that forms the blossom—of nectar-containing flowers.

The common characteristic of hummingbird bills is that they are always relatively thin to allow entry into the flower. Shapes may vary, especially among

FACING PAGE

*Although ranging northward to British Columbia, the black-chinned hummingbird is common only in the southwestern United States, where it exploits nearly forty species of bird-loving flowers.* WAYNE & HELEN LANKINEN

tropical hummingbirds, to probe specific flowers with corollas that are the same shape as the birds' bills. Some have down-curved bills, like the white-tipped sicklebill. More rarely, they may have upturned bills, like the mountain avocetbill. Then there is the singular Andean swordbill hummingbird, which boasts a bill with a 10-centimeter (4-inch) shaft, nearly as long as its body and tail combined. It is adapted to exploit a species of passionflower with a remarkably long corolla tube. All but one North American species, however, have a generalized bill shape, nearly straight and varying in length from 1.4 centimeters (%16 inch) in the male calliope to about 1.9 centimeter (¾ inch) in the female black-chinned. (The southwestern species, Lucifer, has a slightly decurved, or down-turned, bill.) This jack-of-all-trades bill allows temperate species to exploit a greater variety of flowers, an important adaptation for survival in higher latitudes, where plant diversity is not as great as in the tropics.

Like the hummingbird's bill, its tongue is anatomically adapted for divining the nectar wells deep within a flower's corolla. A whitish, translucent organ, the tongue can extend the length of the bill itself beyond the bill tip. It is forced out by the hyoid bones that support the tongue at its base and curve around behind the back of the skull like a coiled clock spring. The tongue is forked midway along its length, and in some species, each prong is fringed on its outer edge. Although these cartilaginous fringes may be caused by normal wear-and-tear, they are thought to help in entraining insects floating in the nectar, and hummingbirds that depend to a greater degree on insects in their diet tend to have more fringes. They also serve in sopping up nectar.

Just how hummingbirds ingest nectar has been a matter of long-standing dispute. At one time, it was thought the hummingbird tongue formed a hollow tube through which the bird sucked the nectar as through a straw. We now know that this is not the case. The outer edges do curl inward, like sheets of rolled paper, to form a double-barreled, trough-like structure. The hummingbird first laps up the nectar, collecting it on the tongue tip, at a rate of ten to fifteen licks per second. The nectar is then drawn passively toward the mouth by capillary action—as any liquid will rise into any such tubular structure—and swallowed in the usual way when the bird retracts the tongue into the beak. In this manner, a hummingbird can consume half its body weight in nectar each day.

## BIRD-LOVING PLANTS

The most compelling question is not how hummingbirds ingest nectar but how and why they came to be nectar eaters in the first place. It is a remarkable story of how hummingbirds and flowers co-evolved, each group to suit its own purpose. For such a co-adapted system to arise and then flourish, both parties must receive a substantial benefit from the relationship. In evolutionary terms, it must confer a better fitness, or survival advantage, to both bird and flower. The flower must increase its chances of being pollinated, and in return, the plant must produce a rich and reliable supply of nectar for the foraging birds.

The system may have come into being when a primitive hummingbird, or swiftlike bird, visited flowers in search of insects and received the extra reward of nectar, a highly desirable avian food for powering flight. This ancestral bird must already have been pre-adapted in some way for nectar feeding, possessing a fine bill and at least a rudimentary ability to hover. At the same time, the plant must have been pre-adapted for bird pollination by its floral structure, the shape of its blossoms, and the position of its sexual organs.

Most hummingbird flowers were originally bee-pollinated. The changeover to bird pollination probably arose at a time when plants were in competition for insect pollination and pollination by birds offered a competitive edge. Karen and Verne Grant, in their classic monograph, *Hummingbirds and Their Flowers,* offer this explanation of the complex evolutionary process:

A plant population adapted for pollination by some class of insects and pre-adapted to hummingbirds, and receiving a greater number of effective pollinating visits by the latter than the former, will be impelled by natural selection to develop floral mechanisms which function more efficiently with the bird visitors. Similarly, the primitive flower visiting hummingbird will be impelled by natural selection to improve its structural and behavioral adaptations for feeding on flowers.

In short, it was a reciprocal relationship, with bird and flower each driving the other toward accommodation and each reaping the benefits of change.

Hummingbird pollination offered some advantages over insect pollination. Perhaps the most obvious advantage for the plant was that hummingbirds could carry larger amounts of pollen on their feathers and bill tips than insects could on their body parts and, therefore, could potentially spread more pollen. The frequent feedings of hummingbirds necessary to power their energetically demanding, hovering flight also meant that the birds visited many flowers daily, increasing the chances of pollination. As well, hummingbirds feed in all kinds of weather, whereas most insects are grounded when it is cold and wet.

Flowers that evolved for bird pollination are called ornithophiles, literally "bird lovers." They have certain characteristics in common, which serve either to attract hummingbirds or, alternatively, to exclude competing pollinators such as bees or butterflies.

Hummingbird flowers are usually large, and either their petals are arrayed parallel to ground level or they hang down, pendant-style, from a flexible stalk. These orientations present no challenge for a hovering hummingbird, which can feed at any angle. For a flower to be pollinated by a bee or butterfly, however, the petals must be arranged facing away from the ground, or if the bloom is horizontal or hanging down, there must be a suitable "landing platform" upon which the insect can alight while extracting nectar. Hummingbird flowers usually lack such structures, discouraging or preventing insect pollination.

The corolla of a bird-loving flower is often trumpet shaped, and the floral tube is of a length and diameter to allow probing by the hummingbird bill and tongue. Measurements show that there is a very strong fit between the length of floral tubes in North American ornithophilous flowers, 15 to 25 millimeters (⅗ to 1 inch), and the length of hummingbird bills. This tube length also makes the nectar inaccessible to all but the long-tongued butterflies and bees. In addition, most hummingbird flowers are odorless, another strategy that excludes insects, as odor serves to attract bees, while hummingbirds lack a sense of smell.

In adapting to hummingbird pollination, the plants have had to gird themselves from injury. As a self-defense mechanism, the corolla in hummingbird flowers is often thickened to prevent the bird's sharp bill from inadvertently puncturing it. Other elements of design shield the sexual organs of the plant, in particular the ovaries, from the feeding bird. In one western North American desert shrub (*Chuparosa*), the style, the slender stalk supporting the stigma, where the pollen is deposited, has a series of ribs that protect the underlying ovary and, at the same time, safely guide the bird's bill to the nectar below the ovary. Experiments in which a sharp needle was repeatedly inserted into the flower showed that at worst the ovary walls were subjected to only harmless, glancing blows.

While protecting itself, the plant must, at the same time, ensure that it is pollinated. For this reason, the nectar is often separated from the anther and stigma— respectively, the pollen-bearing and pollen-receiving organs. Frequently, the anther and stigma protrude from the flower so that as the hummingbird feeds it must first brush by the pollen-containing anthers, which, like fairies' wands, dust pollen on the bird's head, chin, or throat. In one tropical plant, *Marcgravia*, the curving, horn-shaped extension of the nectary forces the hummingbird, after feeding, to hover upward and backward. As it does, its head first brushes by the pollen-bearing anthers and then touches the stigmas of blossoms above where the pollen is deposited, thus completing pollination.

Sometimes, only the bill tip touches the pollen—for example, in some honeysuckles, where the anthers and stigma are hidden within a short floral tube. This type of pollination is less efficient than pollination in other types of ornithophilous flowers, mainly because less pollen is deposited on the bill than on the bird's feathered parts, but also because hummingbirds often clean their bills on twigs after visiting flowers. Scientists believe that plants that use this kind of bill-tip pollination are in a transitional stage in developing adaptations for hummingbird pollination. This type of pollination demonstrates, however, that the co-evolution of birds and flowers is ongoing.

This marvelously adapted win-win system of trumpet-shaped flowers and long-billed pollinators—the hummingbirds—had its origins in the tropics, spreading north when the hummingbirds expanded their ranges.

Today hummingbird flowers are found only in areas where breeding hummingbirds have had enough time to exert selective evolutionary pressure on the plants. The number of bird-loving plants and hummingbird species decreases as you go north. For example, in California there are six species of breeding hummingbirds and eighty species of hummingbird flowers, whereas in Alaska, which only recently emerged from the Ice Age, there is a single hummingbird, the rufous, and only a half-dozen bird-loving flowers.

Some 130 types of hummingbird flowers are found in western North America, where there are seven common hummingbird breeders. Far fewer types of hummingbird flowers, about 30, have been identified east of the Mississippi, where only the ruby-throated hummingbird is a common breeder. Because of recent glaciations in eastern North America, this system of hummingbirds and bird-

*The dominant red color of "bird-loving flowers" acts as a common advertisement, attracting a variety of species, such as this broad-billed hummingbird, and thereby increasing the chances of pollination for all plants in the community.* MARY ANN MCDONALD/BBC NATURAL HISTORY UNIT

pollinated flowers is much simpler, having not had long enough for a high degree of specialization to evolve.

In western North America, the overwhelming number of hummingbird flowers are either perennial herbs or softwood shrubs, which have long blooming seasons. As a result, the nectar supply is available over the breeding and nesting seasons, when the energy demands of the hummingbirds are highest.

There is an added safeguard in this reciprocal system. The common characteristics among hummingbird flowers offer protection for both plant and hummingbird in temperate latitudes. The fact that a plant is not dependent upon a single hummingbird species for pollination, nor the hummingbird upon a single type of plant for nourishment, protects both populations from collapse if calamity befalls one or the other in a particular year.

## DISCRIMINATING TASTES: COLOR AND CONTENT

Perhaps the most obvious characteristic of hummingbird flowers is their dominant red coloration. Why hummingbirds should show a preference for red flowers, or more to the point, why hummingbird flowers should be red in the first place, has been a matter of heated debate and considerable speculation.

Researchers have put forward a number of theories. Some have suggested that hummingbirds are blind to the blue end of the spectrum and thus neglect blue flowers in favor of the more-visible-to-them red flowers. Other scientists have held that red and orange flowers are simply more conspicuous than other colors against a backdrop of greenery. Still others have posited that red is more visible than other colors during the early morning and late evening, when hummingbirds feed most actively.

But do hummingbirds see red better than other colors? Early studies of bird vision did suggest that birds that feed during the day are more stimulated by the red end of the spectrum. However, later experimental evidence did not support the prevailing wisdom that hummingbirds necessarily prefer red to other colors. In a carefully controlled experiment, conducted at the New York Zoological Park in 1950, scientists coated feeders with four colors of nail polish—yellow, green, blue, and red. The position of the feeders was changed every twenty-four hours, and the experiment was conducted over sixteen days to allow for statistical analysis of the three variables—color, position of the feeder, and time of day. The conclusion was disarmingly obvious: the bird, a female green violet-ear, visited the feeder nearest its perch, no matter what color it was—which makes perfect sense, if you think about it. Why drive across town when you can get the same meal next door?

When studying the feeding habits of Mexican hummingbirds, ornithologist Helmuth Wagner also found that an innate preference for red does not exist among hummingbirds in the wild. He set out different-colored feeding flasks in an area where there was also an abundance of natural food sources. He observed that the flask most frequently visited was always the same color as the preferred flower in bloom at that particular season, and this color could be dark blue, purple, or red.

Hummingbirds, it seems, are not attracted to the color red per se but learn by trial and error which types of flowers offer the best sources of nectar and then quickly become conditioned to exploit them.

Nevertheless, most of the bird-loving flowers of North America are indeed red, and that fact demands an explanation. Ecologists have provided us with one, in the theory of convergent evolution, whereby a variety of plants have adopted the same solution to the same problem—how to attract hummingbirds. The dominant color acts literally as a "red flag," a common advertisement among hummingbird flowers that serves all the plants in the community. More than one

species of hummingbird visits the individual plants, allowing all species of plants to share the potential benefits of the hummingbird visitations. The hummingbird species in North America have also converged in the size and shape of their bills, allowing them to exploit most types of hummingbird flowers.

Hummingbirds also benefit from this dominant coloration of hummingbird flowers in that they can quickly recognize new food sources. This ability may be particularly useful during migration, when they have high energy needs and are passing through unfamiliar territory. As David Lazaroff has observed, in *The Secret Lives of Hummingbirds*, the red color serves as "a logo of a fast-food restaurant along the highway." The system prevails over the entire range of hummingbirds, as most hummingbird-pollinated plants in the tropics, where many hummingbirds are not migratory, also have red flowers.

The primary purpose of color, then, seems to be to orient the hummingbird, helping it to home in on potentially rich sources of nectar in its environment, whether temperate or tropical. In the end, however, hummingbirds choose which flowers to return to based not on color but on content. Hummingbirds, it turns out, have discriminating tastes.

Nectars contain three sugars in varying proportions: sucrose, glucose, and fructose. Hummingbirds show a marked preference for nectar rich in sucrose, and nearly all species reject fructose, which, though sweet, has a bitter aftertaste, at least to humans. Virtually all hummingbird flowers in nature have nectars with a high proportion of sucrose; however, among them there is little variability in concentration of sucrose in their nectar. Consequently, hummingbirds tend to exploit those flowers that produce the most nectar and thus reap the richest reward for their effort.

Laboratory studies of hummingbirds' sugar preferences, as well as field observations of flower choice, show that there is a hierarchy of factors influencing their feeding pattern: energy concerns (the volume of nectar flow and concentration

FACING PAGE

*A ruby-throated hummingbird indulges in a drink from a backyard feeder containing a red dye. The use of dyes, implicated in causing cancerous tumors, is strongly discouraged and is unnecessary to attract hummingbirds to feeders.*

ROBERT McCAW

of sugar in the feeder solution) are more important than taste, which indicates the type of sugar. In turn, volume, concentration, and type of sugar are more important than color of the flower or feeder. Put simply, a hummingbird will override its predilection for red flowers if a flower of another color offers richer rewards in energy.

It is significant that flowers adapted for insect pollination have medium-to-low concentrations of sucrose in their nectars, while flowers adapted for hummingbird pollination have nectars relatively rich in sucrose. More than color, these factors—volume of nectar and concentration of sucrose—seem to be the most important adaptations for attracting hummingbirds.

At the same time, the importance of color should not be discounted. The tendency for hummingbird flowers to be red may be another clever evolutionary ploy, relating to the fact that bees see poorly in the red end of the spectrum. Therefore, red functions as yet another exclusion mechanism of bird-loving flowers, favoring their preferred pollinator, the hummingbird.

# LIVING

*Part Two*

# ON THE EDGE

*The prairies, field, orchards and gardens, and even the deepest shades of the forest, are all visited in their turn by this little bird, which everywhere meets with pleasure and food.*

— JOHN JAMES AUDUBON, *The Birds of America* (1840–44)

May 27, 1997, was a very cool and drizzly day—a typical spring day in Maritime Canada. Few flowers were yet in bloom. That morning, my newly returned ruby-throated friend seemed especially active at the feeder. At 11:03, he buzzed into view and I counted as he took twenty-seven sips of the artificial nectar solution. Two minutes later, he was back, supping twenty-eight times on this trip. Two minutes later he was back again, regular as clockwork. To fight the cold and wet, he seemed to need a lot of calories that day, though I lost count of his trips to the feeder.

Energetically, hummingbirds live every day on the edge, between starvation and vigor. This mortal balancing act is the hazard of being so small. In general, the larger the body mass of an animal the more heat that it generates as it burns, or metabolizes, food. Also, the larger the animal the smaller its surface area, through which heat is lost, in relation to its body mass. As a result of this inverse relationship between body mass and surface area, larger animals not only generate more heat

but shed it less quickly than small animals. By contrast, the smaller the animal, the more surface area for its body mass: this relationship translates as greater heat loss for smaller animals, and therefore a critical need to metabolize food quickly and efficiently.

Even though hummingbirds have the most intense metabolic rates ever measured for an animal at rest, because of their small body size they are locked in a constant struggle to maintain a positive energy balance—taking in more energy than they lose. Hummingbirds, along with shrews, probably are at the limits of body size for a warm-blooded creature. If they were any smaller, they simply could not eat enough to balance their heat loss—and they would starve.

Maintaining a positive energy balance is a particular challenge for hummingbirds because of the highly energetic lifestyle associated with their hovering flight. Even when they are resting, their metabolism, as measured by the rate of oxygen consumption, is about twelve times that of a pigeon per gram of body mass. To maintain this rate, their circulatory systems must be highly efficient oxygen-carrying machines. Hummingbirds have the largest known relative heart size of all warm-blooded animals and the most rapid heartbeat, racing at a maximum of 1260 beats per minute in blue-throated hummingbirds. The latter is also a function of size, as a small heart has a short — and therefore fast — stroke. Hummingbirds

*A broad-tailed hummingbird balances on a pencil end. Because of their small size, hummingbirds live every day on the edge, between starvation and vigor—a mortal balancing act.* WENDY SHATTIL/ BOB ROZINSKI

FACING PAGE
*Hummingbird eggs are elongated, white, and extremely small, as indicated by comparison with a dime and a much larger loon egg.* DWIGHT KUHN

have the highest density of red blood cells (6.59 million per cubic millimeter in the ruby-topaz hummingbird) for transporting oxygen to vital organs. As well, their breathing rate is very high, approximately 250 breaths per minute.

Lots of "high-octane" fuel—nectar—is needed to power and maintain this miniature dynamo. A clever series of experiments by Walter Scheithauer demonstrated that not only energy, in the form of sugars, but also protein from insect sources was required to maintain health in hummingbirds. He made available to a white-eared hummingbird a sugar solution of honey. Despite feeding 172 times in a single day, and consuming 80 percent of his body weight in honey, the bird quickly became listless. When an unlimited supply of fruit flies was added to the diet, he consumed 70 percent of his body weight in honey and hawked an average of 677 fruit flies per day, which yielded a mere one-tenth of a gram of protein. The bird, however, was active and alert. Scheithauer concluded that the ideal hummingbird diet, relative to the bird's body weight, was 400 percent water, 70 percent sucrose, 3 percent protein, and 6 percent trace elements. (More recent experiments suggest that a hummingbird need only consume less than double, 164 percent, its own weight in water daily.) He also demonstrated the lightning-quick digestion of hummingbirds. Within ten minutes of ingesting fruit flies, the white-eared hummingbird excreted the insects' chitinous remains. On average it takes an hour for nectar to pass through the digestive tract, and in that time the bird extracts 97 percent of the sugars in the nectar.

It is instructive to compare a hummingbird's metabolism to that of a larger warm-blooded vertebrate such as our own species. If humans were to metabolize food at the same rate as hummingbirds, we would have to consume double our weight every day, or nearly half of our own weight in pure sugar. To accomplish this feat, we would each need to eat 168 kilograms (370 pounds) of potatoes or 59 kilograms (130 pounds) of bread. If such gluttony were possible, weight gain would not be the problem. Human combustion would result as body temperature rose to 400° C (750° F).

## A DAY IN THE LIFE OF A HUMMINGBIRD

To fully appreciate the high-energy lifestyle of hummingbirds, we must examine how they spend their time. A classic study of a day in the life of an Anna's hummingbird gives us an accurate breakdown of the bird's activities in the wild. For two whole days in early September 1953, physiologist Oliver Pearson, stopwatch in hand, kept track of every movement of an Anna's in the botanical gardens of the University of California at Berkeley. The male bird defended a territory only 15 meters (50 feet) in diameter, centered on a fuchsia bush, his nectar source. He left the territory only to chase off other hummingbirds, of either sex, that strayed into his domain.

Pearson found that the bird was especially active in the mornings and in the evenings and relatively inactive during the early afternoon. He flew only 10 percent of the time early in the afternoons but as much as 30 percent of the hour just before dark. Overall, his twenty-four-hour regime could be broken down into three rough categories: daytime perching, flying, and nighttime roosting.

Surprisingly, half of the energy was consumed when the bird was perching—which is what a hummingbird does 80 percent of the time, a fact that belies our image of the bird as a constantly whirring dynamo. But the hummingbird is not sitting around "doing nothing." Recent radioactive isotope experiments demonstrate that when a bird is perching it is emptying its crop, a pouch for storing food between the mouth and the stomach. The bird waits until the crop is about half empty before foraging again. This digestive process takes about four minutes, accounting for the average of fifteen feeding forays an hour.

Although only one-fifth of the Anna's day was spent on the wing, Pearson found that this activity consumed nearly half the bird's energy. He further analyzed the flying time to understand why the bird was in the air. By far the largest part of the flying time was spent on flights to and from the fuchsia bush for nectar. The bird also made short insect-catching forays, a few seconds long, to feed on gnats. He also made an average of fifty flights a day in defense of his territory. These territorial flights consumed 4.5 percent of the bird's energy, which, Pearson calculated, could be furnished by the nectar from just 42 blossoms of the fuchsia. Flights to gather nectar consumed 36 percent of the energy budget, while the insect-catching flights accounted for a minuscule 1.3 percent. Pearson concluded that the single fuchsia bush, with its 1022 blossoms, could supply more than enough nectar to meet the energy needs of the bird. Pearson noted, however, that in September the living was easy for the Anna's hummingbird. Food was abundant, territories were small, and it was a time of relative inactivity as opposed to spring, when the male birds engage in spectacular courtship diving displays, which require extra fuel. During such energetically demanding times, hummingbirds might need to spend more time in the air feeding. They also might need a larger territory to meet their increased energy needs.

## TORPOR: MAKING IT THROUGH THE NIGHT

What happens to hummingbirds at night is perhaps the most intriguing aspect of their total energy picture—how they consume and conserve energy. A byproduct of metabolism is heat, which is shed into the environment. Heat loss becomes a critical issue at night, when hummingbirds can no longer feed. Hummingbirds have a very small capacity for storing energy, and to make matters more precarious, they virtually lack down feathers to insulate themselves from heat loss. Thus, to make it through the night they either must forage more during the day, an activity that could consume as much energy as or more energy than it yields, or they must find a way to use less energy. Hummingbirds have opted for the latter strategy. They lower their temperature at night, entering a state of torpor. This ability to conserve energy, by lowering demand, has allowed hummingbirds to occupy all

FACING PAGE

*A crowned (fork-tailed)*
*woodnymph strikes a*
*dramatic pose.*
*Hummingbirds spend 80*
*percent of the time perching.*
RICHARD R. HANSEN

habitats, from 4000 meters (13,000 feet) in the Andean mountains to sea level elsewhere, and all latitudes, from Alaska to Tierra del Fuego.

Aviculturists had long known that hummingbirds enter torpor, a comalike state accompanied by a lowering of body temperature. Torpid hummingbirds had rarely been observed in the wild, however, until Pearson described his encounter with a torpid Anna's hummingbird that he found, at 3:00 A.M., perched on a branch in his backyard in Oakland, California:

> When picked up he gave a very few slow, wheezy squeaks not unlike those uttered
> by hibernating bats when they are disturbed. He felt slightly warm to the touch,
> but was quite incapable of flight. The air temperature was 15° C. He was carried
> indoors at once to a temperature of 21° C and put on the floor of a cage, but he did
> not revive sufficiently to fly until 3:11. At 7 A.M. he was awake and normally active.

Pearson subsequently kept the bird in captivity for physiological experiments. He observed that the bird entered a seven-hour torpor. In the depths of torpidity, between 1:30 and 3:00 A.M., it was using only ¹⁄₂₈ as much oxygen as during its most active period in the late afternoon. Arousal from the seven-hour-long torpor occurred before daybreak, seemingly spontaneously.

A torpid hummingbird fluffs up its feathers, closes its eyes, and points its bill upward. Over a ninety-minute period one bird's body temperature plunged from 36.4° C (97.5° F) to about 17° C (62.6° F). In another bird, breathing was suspended for five minutes at a body temperature of 9° to 12° C (48.2° to 53.6° F). A bird in normal resting phase at night is using only half as much energy as when it is active during the day. In torpor, it saves an additional 60 to 90 percent of its energy reserves.

The question many biologists had was how often—and under what

*Hummingbirds, such as this recently fledged Anna's, often enter the comalike state of torpor to conserve energy during the night, when they are unable to feed.*
RICHARD R. HANSEN

conditions—do hummingbirds enter torpor? Is it a routine practice or an emergency measure only? Much of the pioneering work to answer these questions has been done at the Rocky Mountain Biological Laboratory near Gothic, Colorado. One of North America's leading hummingbird biologists, William Calder, of the University of Arizona, has studied the phenomenon in broad-tailed hummingbirds, a high-country species. At 3000 meters (10,000 feet), temperatures during the breeding season range from $-6°$ to $+25°C$ ($19°$ to $77°F$). Under the freezing conditions that can occur here, it might well be necessary for hummingbirds to enter torpor to balance their energy expenditures and, literally, make it through the night.

Over four consecutive summers Calder documented the feeding behavior of broad-tailed hummingbirds. In preparation for nighttime, they seemed to alter their feeding pattern. Calder observed that at dusk male hummingbirds increased both the size and frequency of their feeding bouts, adding one-third to their body weight before flying up the mountainside to their nighttime roosts. Females, who remained on nests at lower altitudes, were also observed to tank up at dusk.

During daytime feeding, the birds gradually gain weight, converting sugar to fat. Also, they store nectar in their crop as an additional energy reserve. When temperatures plunge, however, as they can do early in the breeding season in the mountains, hummingbirds may also have to become torpid to stretch their energy reserves until morning.

But Calder observed that torpor was by no means a nightly affair. Only birds that had come up short on their daytime feeding, because of storm conditions, for example, and therefore did not accumulate a normal energy reserve by nightfall, seemed to resort to torpor.

At one time, it was thought that during torpor the birds abandoned control of their body temperature, and that it went into a free-fall, conforming closely to the

FACING PAGE

*A study showed that a male Anna's spent 36 percent of its energy on nectar-gathering flights.*

WAYNE & HELEN LANKINEN

HUMMINGBIRDS USE

TORPOR WHENEVER

THEY ARE

ENERGETICALLY

STRESSED—FOR

EXAMPLE, WHEN BAD

WEATHER LIMITS

FORAGING OR WHEN

ENERGY SOURCES ARE

SCARCE.

ambient environmental temperature. Scientists now know that the process of torpor is self-regulating. The Andean hillstar, which roosts at night in Peruvian caves on the cold Andean plateau, maintains its temperature at 7° C (44.6° F), the minimum body temperature from which spontaneous arousal has been observed, despite lower air temperatures. Most hummingbird species, however, regulate their body temperature at 18° to 20° C (64.4° to 68° F), regardless of the temperature outside.

This internal regulatory mechanism acts much as a fuel gauge does. If the gauge reads low, because of a shortfall in the day's feeding, the bird will enter torpor. However, there is no magic threshold—no set reading on the fuel gauge— below which birds automatically become torpid. It varies with circumstances. During migration, for instance, the threshold is set much higher to conserve fat for the journey ahead. On occasion, tragically, the fuel gauge malfunctions, or environmental conditions are simply too extreme to counteract. After a frosty night, my neighbors found a resident ruby-throat dead on the ground below its powerline perch, where apparently it had died of hypothermia.

Just as hummingbirds have a biological fuel gauge, initiating torpor when energy reserves are in danger of depletion, hummingbirds also seem to possess an internal biological clock that is timed for a first-light search for more food. Light intensity triggers the bird's arousal and the rapid return of body temperature to normal.

If the outside temperature falls below 18° C (64.4° F), hummingbirds consume more oxygen to maintain body temperature at that level and thus minimize arousal time (about 1 minute per degree C change in body temperature). This adaption is an important safeguard to prevent predation and to improve the bird's competitive advantage for food. This strategy seems to be an evolutionary compromise between energy conservation and other factors important to the bird's survival.

This remarkable self-regulating process not only is admirable from a physiological viewpoint but could serve as a model for our own management of resources. As William Calder has observed:

> Tiny hummingbirds, nesting in the chilling nocturnal climate of the Rocky Mountains, are succeeding in near marginal energetic conditions. A reduction in feeding opportunity by inclement weather or by demands of nest protection may lead to an energy crisis. Unlike man, the nesting hummingbird reduced the rate of depletion of energy reserves, rather than crying for more.

In general, it seems that the emergency-only hypothesis of torpor prevails. Hummingbirds use torpor whenever they are energetically stressed—for example, when bad weather limits foraging or when energy sources are scarce. There is now evidence that hummingbirds also use torpor as a way of conserving energy stored as fat in preparation for migration, a time of great energy need for all birds.

University of California biologist F. Lynn Carpenter and Mark Hixon, of Oregon State University, uncovered this function of torpor when studying rufous hummingbirds, which breed as far north as Alaska and winter in Mexico. Rufous hummingbirds undertake the longest migrations of any hummingbird—up to 3000 kilometers (1900 miles)—in proportion to their size the longest migration of any bird in the world.

They migrate from July to September through the mountains of the western United States, stopping en route to feed in alpine meadows, where they replenish their fat stores. Studies carried out in the eastern Sierra Nevada show that they stop to refuel at a weight of 3.3 grams and over a week bulk up on nectar to a weight of 4.5 to 5.6 grams—a 25 to 40 percent weight increase. Practically all of the hummingbirds' weight gain is in the form of fat, which accumulates in a smooth layer beneath the skin, on the back and breast, and at the base of the neck. Once they have laid down sufficient reserves, they continue their migration, buzzing into the sky early in the morning.

Carpenter and Hixon had a rare opportunity to observe an immature male in torpor when he roosted on an exposed willow branch near his feeding territory. She had been monitoring this bird during his migratory stopover and knew that he was a normal, healthy bird who was not energetically stressed. Nevertheless, within forty-five minutes after roosting, he entered a torpid state, fluffing his feathers, thrusting his beak skyward, and becoming insensitive to stimuli around him, including the flashlights, electronic flashes, and noises made by the researchers as they photographed him. The bird remained torpid throughout the night, a strategy not predicted for a fat, healthy bird. Furthermore, Carpenter reasoned, if the bird had been energetically stressed, it would seem unlikely that he would choose such an exposed location, where heat loss would be more rapid.

Carpenter proposed that the function of torpor in this individual was the conservation of energy reserves for migratory flight. She calculated that the bird saved about 10 percent of his total fat reserve by assuming torpor. Such a fuel-saving strategy may be common among migrating rufous hummingbirds. If so, it may point to a different physiological trigger for torpor from low blood sugar or fat levels only. It seems that the bird somehow re-calibrates its fuel gauge to a higher setting, in preparation for its energetically demanding journey.

As dawn approached the rufous hummingbird began to arouse. At 5:45, he stretched and five minutes later flew south and was not seen again.

## FOLLOWING THE FLORAL HIGHWAY

Rufous hummingbirds follow an elliptical migratory pattern, passing though the Colorado desert and along the lowlands and foothills of the Pacific slope of the

FACING PAGE

*While feeding at a monkey flower, a broad-tailed hummingbird fans its namesake retrices, or tail feathers, which are longer than those in many other related species.*
WENDY SHATTIL/
BOB ROZINSKI

FIGURE 2

*Migratory pattern of*

*rufous hummingbirds.*

ADAPTED FROM W. A. CALDER,

1993, *RUFOUS HUMMINGBIRD*,

THE BIRDS OF NORTH

AMERICA, NO. 53

(PHILADELPHIA: THE

ACADEMY OF NATURAL

SCIENCES).

Coast range in early spring on their trip north and returning on a more easterly course in the fall, along the western mountain ranges. There are two southbound flyways, passing either side of the Great Basin desert, one along the Coast ranges and the Sierra Nevada and the other following the Rocky Mountain Cordillera (Figure 2).

The birds' movements seem to be in synchrony with blooming of hummingbird flowers: they follow a floral highway. The spring migration proceeds more slowly, probably as a precautionary measure to avoid overshooting the leading edge of spring's advance and thus arriving at a destination where nectar is in short supply or, worse, is unavailable. An energetically demanding undertaking such as migration is always fraught with danger and sometimes ends in disaster. The birds must fly over western deserts and grasslands when nectar-bearing flowers may not be in bloom and water may not be available. One researcher saw a migrant rufous hummingbird fall from the sky in the Mojave where there was neither water nor nectar. Eventually, most rufous hummingbirds do reach their breeding grounds in the Pacific Northwest, some penetrating into southern Yukon and Alaska.

By July, these northern breeders are already headed south. The reasons for their southerly route through the mountains relate, at least in part, to the availability of food. Heavy summer rains in the mountains ensure a supply of flowering plants. Bird-pollinated flowers in the alpine meadows are said to occur in "flocks"—five or six species together—whereas the bird-pollinated species that occur in spring and late winter on the adjacent lowlands do so singly or in pairs. The buffet of flowers in the mountains attracts several species of hummingbirds. In California's high Sierra Nevada, calliope, rufous, and Allen's hummingbirds are often seen feeding together.

The synchrony between the blooming of bird-pollinated flowers in eastern North America and the migratory pattern of ruby-throated hummingbirds is not

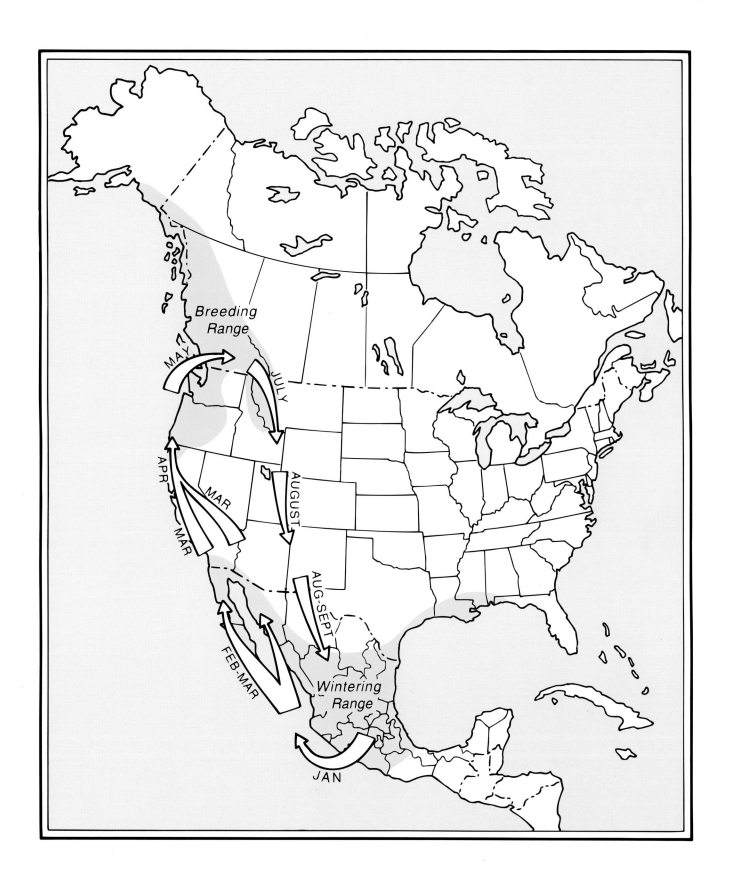

as well developed. There are some thirty bird-pollinated plants in the ruby-throat's range but none precisely overlap with it. But the ruby-throat's range in the east coincides, to a striking degree, with the extent of the eastern deciduous and mixed forests on the continent. Not only is this habitat rich in flowering plants, it also provides an alternative food source, in the form of sap.

INITIATE MIGRATION.

In spring, throughout the ruby-throat's range, peak migration precedes the peak flowering time for most bird-pollinated plants. Ruby-throats compensate by hawking insects—never in short supply in the north woods!—and for quick energy they seem to rely on sap, a readily available sugar source in their woodland habitat. Ruby-throats are frequently seen buzzing around yellow-bellied sapsuckers and pirating sap from sapsucker wells.

In the fall, however, there is one plant that seems to be in sync with the ruby-throat's movements. Peak flowering of jewelweed (*Impatiens* sp.) consistently occurs a few days before peak fall migration across the ruby-throat's vast range. The abundance of jewelweed, the hummingbirds' heavy use of it, and the relative scarcity of other fall-blooming hummingbird plants suggest that it has a strong influence on the timing of ruby-throat migration.

## FRONTS, MOUNTAINS, AND GULFS: OTHER FACTORS IN HUMMINGBIRD MIGRATION

One day in late August, the familiar hum of my resident ruby-throats is not heard. The feeder hangs, full but unattended. My hummingbirds, answering to their own hormonal urges and the external cues of light and weather, have decided it is time to go. They have flown, gone south for another season to their winter home in Mexico or Central America.

If I had been attending more closely to the weather, I might have predicted the day of their departure. Like most avian migrants, hummingbirds take advantage

FACING PAGE
*A calliope hummingbird extracts sap from a sapsucker well in Alberta. Sap is an important alternative food supply to nectar, especially in more northerly latitudes.*
ROBERT McCAW

of favorable weather patterns to initiate migration. Typically, they follow the passage of cold fronts that bring strong northwest winds. En route, they also use the north-south line of the Appalachian Mountains as a migratory map. By the time I noticed they were gone, my hummingbirds were winging their way across the ridges of this old mountain range that stretches from Maritime Canada south to Alabama.

In the 1980s, research atop the Appalachian lookout at Hawk Mountain Sanctuary, Pennsylvania, showed that the migration of ruby-throated hummingbirds spans the period from August 8 through September 25, with numbers peaking in the last week of August. More hummingbirds were observed when winds blew from the north than from the south. In addition, the numbers of hummingbirds increased significantly with wind speed, suggesting that the birds were taking advantage of tailwinds. Researchers also noted that hummingbirds were seen flying south more frequently during the midday hours than at other times, an observation in agreement with an earlier study on the Allegheny Front of West Virginia. It may be that hummingbirds must use the early hours of the day to replenish energy reserves depleted during the night, and that they must use the hours before dusk to tank up before fasting for the night.

The migratory period of ruby-throated hummingbirds is much shorter than that of western species, such as the calliope and rufous hummingbirds, which make extended refuelling stops in the alpine meadows of the Rockies on their way south. The ruby-throats' shortened migratory season, along with observations of midday flying, suggests that they migrate in "short-hop" flights. One ruby-throat was banded in Oklahoma and recaptured, thirty-two days later, in Texas. The distance between the two points was 760 kilometers (470 miles), indicating the bird covered an average of 23.75 kilometers (14.75 miles) per day.

Ruby-throats do make remarkable long-distance flights, however. For many

FACING PAGE

*Hummingbirds generally prefer the rich diversity of mountain habitats, such as this cloud forest in Henri Pittier Park, Venezuela, to lowland habitats. In winter, migrants and resident birds must share resources.*

JONATHAN GRANT

*A tufted croquette, native to southeastern South America, displays its brilliant crown and gorget feathers. As with many birds, male hummingbirds are the showiest, an advertisement intended to attract the attention of the female.*
ART WOLFE

years, there was controversy about whether or not ruby-throats cross the Gulf of Mexico on their way to wintering grounds in Mexico. Original calculations of the energetics of such a marathon flight suggested that it was not possible. However, reports persisted of hummingbirds overflying the gulf. Shrimp boat crews saw ruby-throated hummingbirds skimming above the waves, 100 kilometers (60 miles) from land. Occasionally, exhausted hummingbirds perched on oil-drilling rigs, 330 kilometers (200 miles) from shore. One simple explanation was that these birds had been blown offshore by the strong winds that prevail in the gulf. The other theory was that hummingbirds deliberately overfly these waters. The shortest distance across the gulf is 735 kilometers (457 miles), a seemingly insurmountable and potentially deadly obstacle. More recent and sophisticated measurements of the flight capacity of ruby-throats suggest that the birds could fly 975 kilometers (600 miles) on 2 grams of fat, enabling them to cross the gulf without the benefit of tailwinds.

When birder Ted Eubanks lived along the upper Texas coast, he frequently witnessed the spring arrival of ruby-throats from over the gulf. It appears that these hummers regularly traverse the gulf in spring. There is evidence, however, that in the fall, many hummers hug the coast, making their way to Mexico via Mississippi, Alabama, Louisiana, and Texas. Large numbers of hummers are seen each year along the Coastal Bend, near Rockport, Texas, where the Hummer/Bird Celebration is held each fall. Instead of overflying the gulf or following this overland route, other birds island hop from Key West, Florida, to Cuba, a distance of 160 kilometers (90 miles); then, cross the Yucatán Channel from the western tip of Cuba, a longer leap of 200 kilometers (120 miles).

However a ruby-throat accomplishes this leg of the journey, the migration of a bird weighing a little better than 3 grams over a total distance of 2500 kilometers (1550 miles) is an impressive feat.

When the short-billed migrant hummingbirds of North America arrive in the tropics to spend the winter months, they must share the resources there with the resident hummingbirds. Fortunately, the dry season in the tropics, which occurs when it is winter in the north, is also the time of sexual reproduction for trees and shrubs—and thus the time of most abundant flowering. Studies carried out in the states of Colima and Jalisco, on the west coast of Mexico, demonstrate that there is an abundance of food, more than enough to feed both residents and migrants. At the same time, feeding is not free of competition. There is a clear hierarchy among the hummingbirds, native and newly arrived, for access to the best and sweetest flowers.

Hummingbirds that dwell year-round in the tropics (so-called endemics) fall into two distinct groups: the residents and the wanderers. Residents occupy the same habitat year-round, even when the number of flowers dwindles. Wanderers, like hovering gypsies, move from one habitat to another, following the seasonal blooms of trees and shrubs. When migrants invade the tropics for a brief four months, territorial skirmishes with both residents and wanderers are inevitable.

In this struggle for resources, the residents are dominant, monopolizing the best territories. They appropriate the high-nectar-producing tubular flowers, aggressively defending them. Curiously, they even continue to feed on these prime flowers at times of low nectar production. It seems, to borrow a phrase, they would rather fight than switch. In Colima, the long-tailed hermit, cinnamon hummingbird, amethyst-throated hummingbird, and magnificent hummingbird are the most dominant resident species.

Wanderers spend more time at cup-shaped flowers that are lower in nectar content but are often abundant. The migrants must take potluck. Fortunately, the cup-shaped

flowers bloom prolifically in highland habitats, on the floor of montane forests, providing a surplus of nectar for migrants and wanderers. Although migrants will vigorously defend these marginal areas, low-dominance, smaller species, such as the ruby-throated, calliope, and Allen's hummingbirds, often become fugitives, as they are driven out of even low-value territories and forced to seek out unoccupied ones.

Despite this competition for the best resources, the overall productivity of the tropics ensures that all the species glean enough to meet their needs. When flowers are not in bloom, as they often are not when the North American migrants first arrive, they survive almost exclusively on a diet of insects. Insects also comprise 60 percent of the their diet just before the birds depart for northern breeding grounds.

Fifteen years of observations in the Monteverde Cloud Forest Reserve in Costa Rica, carried out by Northern Arizona University biologist Peter Feinsinger, has yielded a more complete and complex picture of how hummingbirds work out the sharing of resources. The birds can be categorized according to their methods of procuring or protecting their food supply. The most prominent groups, or feeding guilds, are territorialists and trapliners; then there are the more clandestine groupings of marauders, filchers, and piercers that collectively might be described as territory parasites.

Territorialists, as the name suggests, vigorously defend a patch of nectar-bearing flowers. One such territorialist is the purple-throated mountain gem. Part of its defensive arsenal is its namesake gorget, which flashes a warning in frequent head-to-head confrontations with other hummers that would impinge on its feeding territory.

Not all hummingbirds are involved in such territorial games of hide-and-seek or thrust-and-parry. The trapliner has adopted the strategy of visiting a series of flowers of different species along a prescribed line or route—much in the manner

ON OCCASION, THE

NORMAL, INTENSE

INTERSPECIES

RIVALRY AMONG

HUMMINGBIRDS

DISSOLVES AND TWO

SPECIES WORK OUT A

SEEMINGLY COZY

RELATIONSHIP,

DIVVYING UP A FOOD

SOURCE INTO

DISCRETE NICHES.

of a fur trapper who tends a line of traps. Some hummingbirds, such as the green hermit and long-tailed hermit, have specialized curved bills to exploit flowers with similar corolla shapes—a case of co-evolution. These flowers, however, are often spread out under the forest canopy rather than concentrated in a patch that could be defended. These specialized feeders are known as high-reward trapliners. The low-reward trapliners have smaller, straighter bills and are more generalized foragers, often visiting more than one species of flower. From the plant's viewpoint, this feeding strategy might seem to be counterproductive, as the pollen might be wasted on a different species. But flowers frequented by low-reward trapliners have evolved an ingenious solution to this potential problem; they are constructed so that they transfer the pollen to a particular part of the hummingbird's anatomy— its bill, crown, or throat. When the hummingbird feeds on another flower of the same species, it too is structured so that it is fertilized in the process.

The territory parasites must secure a meal at the expense of the territorialists. Marauders are usually large species that simply barge into a territory, like the proverbial school yard bullies or local thugs, and take what they want, despite the territorialists' frantic efforts to repel them. Filchers are usually smaller than marauders and must exercise more stealth. They lurk around the edges of a territory, darting in when the defender is busy fending off another intruder. Among the most adept of filchers are the magenta-throated woodstars. They are so small and their buzzing flight so similar to that of bees that they are often mistaken for these insects by other hummingbirds, allowing them to steal in, in full view of the territorialist.

A final class of territory parasite, the piercer, depends upon a kind of subterfuge to gain its nectar reward, with no discernible benefit to the plant. The stripe-tailed hummingbird uses its needle-sharp bill, which is too short to reach the nectar well of a tubular corolla, to pierce the base of long-tubed flowers, siphoning off the nectar without ever touching the stamens or stigmas.

On occasion, the normal, intense interspecies rivalry among hummingbirds dissolves and two species work out a seemingly cozy relationship, divvying up a food source into discrete niches. Helmuth Wagner, in his classic study, "Food of Mexican Hummingbirds," observed an example of this resource partitioning on the Pacific coast of Chiapas. Near his camp there was an enormous leafless tree in full bloom. Every evening and morning, it was filled with cinnamon hummingbirds and green-breasted mangos, a bronze-green hummingbird that occurs on both slopes of the mountainous spine of Mexico and Central America. Wagner observed that the two species divided the tree between them: the cinnamon hummingbirds took charge of the lower branches of the tree, while the green-breasted mangos occupied the top section. This seemingly passive relationship was not without strife, however; if either species strayed across the invisible boundary line between their feeding territories, it was immediately driven back to its own side. The cinnamon hummingbird was observed to have a similar relationship with the steely-vented hummingbird in the Guanacaste area; the cinnamon hummingbird worked the lower sections of the tree and outside of the crown, while the smaller steely-vented exploited the interior of the tree. As the dominant species, the larger cinnamon hummingbirds sometimes drove off their smaller neighbors.

Wherever hummingbirds are found, in the tropics, on northern breeding grounds, or somewhere in between during migration, they must wage a constant struggle to secure enough energy to sustain their high-energy, high-risk lifestyle.

*A female rufous
hummingbird feeds from
a columbine. The pollen-
bearing anthers often project
from the corollas of
hummingbird flowers, where
they dust pollen on the bird's
head, chin, or throat.*
WAYNE & HELEN LANKINEN

65

# HOME LIFE

*Part Three*

# OF HUMMERS

*I wish it were in my power to impart to you the delight I have felt while watching a pair of these most favorite little creatures displaying their feelings and love for each other.*

— JOHN JAMES AUDUBON, *The Birds of America* (1840–44)

It is May 20, 1998, a year to the day since I hailed the arrival of my first hummingbird of the previous spring. As an act of faith and welcome, I have hung my feeder, with its four parts water to one part sugar. It swings gently in the spring breeze as I look out, expectantly, for the first bright flash of red, the whir of wings.

Now, at 11:30 A.M., a hummer has arrived, a female, supping long at the feeder. After tanking up, she buzzes off toward the apple tree, where she perches among the first flush of pink-and-white blossoms. Through my scope, I watch as she flexes her wings, shakes her tail, and strops her beak on a branch—commonplace behaviors that nevertheless enlarge my day.

Normally, the first hummer to arrive is a male. This is no accident but an evolutionary strategy designed to increase the fitness of the species. By migrating first, the male follows the advance of spring northward and therefore he becomes the one—not the female—to risk overshooting the food supply, a real possibility here at the far northern reaches of the ruby-throat's breeding range. And if the

FACING PAGE

*A long-billed starthroat of Venezuela broods in its elaborately constructed and camouflaged nest.*

ART WOLFE

male should fall, it is little loss to the species, as all male hummingbirds are promiscuous and they contribute very little, if anything, to the raising of the young. Not so with the females, upon whom the reproductive capacity of the species depends. The females, therefore, trail the wave of early male hummingbirds, returning to their nesting site with fidelity when the blossoms are starting to burst forth.

I assume that a prospective male mate is already on territory, and that I have simply not yet seen him. When he arrives on the scene he will engage in his usual rough-house behavior, driving all other hummers, even females with whom he will try to mate, away from what he asserts is his feeder.

Throughout the spring and summer, I can look forward to watching the resident hummingbirds as they shuttle back and forth to the feeder and engage in vigorous territorial defense. But like most other hummingbird watchers, I will be lucky to observe the more intimate details of the birds' domestic lives—their mating and the subsequent raising of young—especially as ruby-throats are rarely backyard nesters, preferring the protection of the deep woods.

## COURTSHIP ANTICS: SONG ASSEMBLIES AND WING WHISTLES

Hummingbirds engage in elaborate courtship antics. Whereas many male birds, principally songbirds, advertise their availability to a mate with song, hummingbirds are weak voiced—for the most part, uttering only a series of chattering, unmusical squeaks. For most, then, song is not an effective advertisement. Instead, they play to their strengths: brilliant color and aerial genius.

An exception to this rule is the hermit group of tropical hummingbirds. Their use of song, such as it is, seems to relate to their breeding environment. Hermits inhabit dense rain-forest habitat where visual displays would be ineffective. As well, hermits themselves are generally brownish, drab-colored creatures in

FACING PAGE

*A blue-throated hummingbird often spreads its white-tipped tail feathers in flight. Males frequently form leks, or singing assemblies, to attract females.* RUSSELL C. HANSEN/IVY IMAGES

comparison with their flashier brethren and therefore make less fetching avian billboards. They counter these disadvantages by forming song assemblies, joining their voices in a common chorus. Such assemblies may consist of as few as two or three individuals, or as many as a hundred birds.

The courtship crooning is concerted and persistent in some species. Trinidad little hermits, for example, form assemblies for an eight-month period extending from November until the post-breeding molt in July. During this time, a male may spend as much as 70 percent of the daylight hours on his singing perch, singing every two seconds, or twelve thousand times a day.

The songs of each assembly are different; in effect, they comprise a song dialect, suggesting that they are learned. The areas where these discrete courtship assemblies take place are called leks, and females visit these all-male choirs for the sole purpose of mating. Long-tailed hermits may maintain leks at the same site for as long as twelve years. Such territories appear to serve as mating stations only, as they are not rich enough in nectar-bearing flowers to serve as self-sufficient feeding territories.

Within a lek, dominant males usually occupy a central territory, while subordinate hopefuls are relegated to the margins. Since the dominant males must leave the lek to forage, these marginalized males also have a window of opportunity to mate with visiting females.

Different mating strategies are used in the more open breeding habitat that generally prevails in North America. Here, visual display is dominant over the use of song. Sound, principally produced by wing and tail feathers, plays an important part in the mating behavior of some species, however, including Costa's, rufous, Allen's, and broad-tailed hummingbirds.

The female controls the timing of mating, seeking out a mate only after she has finished building a nest. The courtship consists of two phases. First, the male lures the female with a species-specific plumage display. Then male and female perform a nuptial flight, culminating in copulation.

During the luring phase, males often perform elaborate dive displays, which produce a characteristic "wing whistle" as air rushes through the slots between their primary feathers. It is extremely difficult to determine whether these displays are primarily territorial, or primarily for sexual attraction. Most biologists believe that they are probably a bit of both. The main function appears to be territorial, but they may have the side benefit of attracting a female, who may tend to mate with those males who are most dominant or conspicuous. When broad-tailed hummingbirds were silenced experimentally, they tended to lose their territories to rival hummingbirds. Ultimately, loss of the wing whistle, which serves as a threat, affected their reproductive success.

Male broad-tailed hummingbirds have also been shown to purposely limit their food intake to avoid compromising their aerial performance. They maintain this training weight by ingesting only 14 percent of their crop capacity in the mornings and then feeding intensively at dusk, ingesting 179 percent of their crop capacity—enough to preclude the need to enter torpor without increasing their daytime weight. The imperative to perform well, chasing other males away and showing off for females with a series of power dives, seems to override even their own need to ensure adequate energy reserves, a dramatic example of voluntary weight control and avian macho behavior.

Males on a breeding territory are notoriously aggressive. Even when a female first appears on a male's territory, the male usually attempts to drive her away, treating her as he would another intruding male. Some biologists believe that males attain copulation by intimidation rather than by the finer art of courtship. This aggressive display, however, may be viewed as an initial phase of courtship.

Two North American species, Anna's and Costa's hummingbirds, engage in

particularly elaborate courtships. When a female Anna's hummingbird enters a male's core breeding territory, the male will give chase. If the female perches, the male immediately initiates its dive display, "the most elaborate and spectacular dive display of any North American hummingbird," according to ornithologist F. Gary Stiles. The whole show lasts a scant twelve seconds. The male first sings a set of buzzy notes; then he climbs nearly vertically for seven or eight seconds to a height of 20 to 40 meters (65 to 130 feet) before plummeting in a nearly vertical dive to within a meter of the perched female. His daredevil dive climaxes with a loud dive noise, which may be entirely vocal or entirely or partly produced by wing vibrations (yet another bone of contention among hummingbird researchers). He completes his dive by hovering at the starting point. It is significant that the male always orients himself during this loop-to-loop so that the sun reflects from his brilliant rose gorget and crown toward the object of his desire. If the female is suitably impressed, she will lead the male toward her nesting area, where she again perches.

The male then begins a second series of maneuvers, which may include high-intensity singing or a shuttle display, or both. The high-intensity song, which may last several minutes without a break, consists of a rapid buzzing composed of some 110 to 115 syllables per second. As he sings, he engages in back-and-forth shuttle flights, above or in front of the female, effectively pinning her to the perch. The female tracks the male with her bill. If she does not fly, the encounter may end in copulation at the completion of the high-intensity song. The male mounts the female's back with wings whirring, sometimes seizing her crown feathers with his bill. The brief act lasts only three to five seconds.

The Costa's hummingbird has an even more impressive repertoire of courtship moves, consisting of four distinct aerial displays. In the looping dive-and-whistle, the male flies toward the perched female and then climbs steeply while emitting a very high thin vocalization, colorfully described by one nineteenth-century naturalist

FEMALE AND THEN

CLIMBS STEEPLY WHILE

EMITTING A VERY HIGH

THIN VOCALIZATION,

COLORFULLY DESCRIBED

BY ONE NINETEENTH-

CENTURY NATURALIST

AS "A SOUND LIKE THE

HIGHEST AND SHARPEST

NOTE THAT CAN BE

MADE ON A VIOLIN."

as "a sound like the highest and sharpest note that can be made on a violin." At the top of the arc, he slows momentarily, changes the plane of the loop, and then plummets, passing within a few meters of the female. At the bottom of the loop, the wings produce a noise that one early-twentieth-century naturalist, M. L. Dawson, described as "the very shrillest [sound] in the bird world, and one which is fairly terrifying in its intensity…like the shriek of a glancing bullet, or a bit of shrapnel." Without pausing, the Costa's male climbs into another loop and may continue the display for two to four minutes, though commonly he persists for thirty seconds only.

Although copulation has never been observed immediately following such displays, they probably convey information about the condition and age of the male. Juveniles appear unable to carry off these daredevil acrobatics with perfection and do not have adult vocal capability—tip-offs that would cause females to reject such immature mating partners.

Costa's hummingbirds also have a version of the shuttle display, called close-range flight. The male hovers within a meter of the female, sometimes "pouncing"—moving up and down—other times shuttling, back and forth. This up-close-and-personal display shows to best effect the male's iridescent purple crown and flared gorget, and it is thought that it is more closely linked with copulation than the looping dive-and-whistle, which nevertheless serves as an attention-getter. The close-range flight is even more energetically demanding, since the bird must beat his wings very rapidly to maintain position, and therefore is much shorter than the dive-and-whistle display.

Copulation in this species has only been documented once, in mesquite brush, in Joshua Tree National Park. The male flew toward the female in short, darting flight, mounted her while she perched, and then, in the words of the observers, "the two buzzed off in close pursuit."

Males generally mate with more than one female. After copulation, the male

FACING PAGE

*A female ruby-throat sits on her well-camouflaged nest. Ruby-throats usually build their nests over water as protection from terrestrial predators.* ROGER ERIKSSON

buzzes off for good. Once he has passed on his genetic material, the male hummingbird's job is done. Males take no part in the rearing of the young, leaving all of the rearing duties to the females. Paul Johnsgard, author of *The Hummingbirds of North America*, has observed, "No other major avian family seems to have adopted so overwhelmingly this trend toward male emancipation from nesting responsibilities and consequent promiscuous mating tendencies." He concludes that this "devil-may-care mating system" is yet another component of the hummingbird's high-risk, high-reward lifestyle.

Rare exceptions to this pattern have been reported. Both ruby-throated and rufous hummingbirds have been observed to take part in incubation, though the individuals in question may have been masculinized females. These two species are the most northerly breeding hummingbirds, suggesting that there may be an advantage in the male's participation in incubation and brooding as a hedge against the harsher climactic conditions and limited food resources in northern latitudes.

There is also a single reported case of a male Anna's hummingbird feeding young, after their mother vanished just before the nestlings fledged. Anna's hummingbirds, which are nonmigratory, can encounter harsh climatic conditions. Alone among North American hummingbirds, they breed in the winter months, January to April, "sometimes amid frost and snow," according to Skutch. In California chaparral habitat, they time their breeding cycle to the onset of winter rains, which brings forth the blooms of the chaparral currant. By breeding early, they also avoid competition with other temperate hummingbird species who share their breeding habitat. In California, fledging occurs between March and June, when the flowering of gooseberry peaks.

Whether in the tropics or more temperate zones, hummingbirds choose the season of peak flowering to initiate the breeding cycle. In Central America, Skutch observed that local breeders nest in the first part of the dry season, October to

February, when the earth retains sufficient moisture and sunny skies "call forth a profusion of bright blossoms." A study carried out in Guadalupe Canyon, in southern New Mexico and Arizona, also showed that breeding hummingbirds—black-chinned, broad-billed, violet-crowned, and Costa's—chose nesting sites where nectar was most available.

## GOSSAMER CONNECTIONS

On a visit to the Hummingbird Aviary at the Arizona–Sonora Desert Museum on the outskirts of Tucson, I watched as an Anna's hummingbird buzzed at ankle height along the cobbled footpath. It seemed strange to see a hummingbird at my feet, until I noticed the business that occupied this low-flying hummer. It was plucking strands of cobwebs that clung to the interstices of stone lining the pathway. I watched as it buzzed away, like a tiny, busy tailor, trailing the silvery thread in its needlelike bill. While hovering—an ability critical to the task—it will weave this gossamer but hardy material into its tiny nest, using it as a cable to gird and bind the structure together. Cobwebs have a second virtue beyond their deceptive strength, their plasticity. The female shapes the nest from the inside, to conform closely to her own body shape, and later the nest will expand to accommodate growing chicks.

The hummingbird nest has been variously praised as "one of the daintiest structures in the world," "among the most remarkable of all avian structures,"and "a model of artistic workmanship," and, more mundanely, by the pioneer ornithologist Alexander Wilson, as "a mere mossy knot." Most North American hummingbird nests are similar in design. Small cups, which have an inside diameter of 3.75 to 5.0 centimeters (1.5 to 2.0 inches) and which are 2.5 centimeters (1 inch) deep, they are wrapped in spider web or other silken material. The inside of the nest is lined with soft materials, frequently the cottony seed of a plant or feather down, for insulation and to cushion the eggs. Usually, as a final touch, bits of lichen, bark, or moss are stuck to the outside surface for camouflage. The female may complete the work in a day or two, if she is energetically fit, but more frequently nest building occupies a week, and she may continue to add materials throughout the incubation period. Anna's hummingbirds follow this practice, creating what naturalist Robert S. Woods once described as "the most beautiful of all the hummingbird nests."

"Often eggs are laid in the nest when it is a mere platform," writes Woods, "and the remaining part of the nest is built up around the eggs and the finishing touches of lichens and plant seed put on last."

As I walked along the pathway at the aviary, I came upon a brooding Anna's, her nest sequestered deep within the lattice of a dense shrub. Her bill and tail poked out from either side of the well-camouflaged nest at the same jaunty, 45-degree angle—sticking up like old-fashioned television "rabbit ears." The nest was constructed at a fork of what seemed to me a very fragile branch, about the circumference of my little finger. It was, as Woods claimed, a "most beautiful" nest, with the outside decorated with what appeared to be a garland of dried white blossoms.

According to reports compiled by Arthur Cleveland Bent, hummingbirds have also been known to build nests in a bizarre variety of unlikely settings: "…on a porch where doors were swinging open at all hours of the day and night, on a steel rod poked into the roof of a blacksmith shop where men were busy at an anvil, and on an old piece of haywire stuck into a chink in the wall of a barn." The nest builder in this last example was the black-chinned hummingbird, which normally prefers sycamore trees in canyons with flowering sage close by and in willow thickets near streams or lakes. Its close relative, the ruby-throat, commonly builds its nest on a down-sloping branch over water, presumably as a defensive strategy against

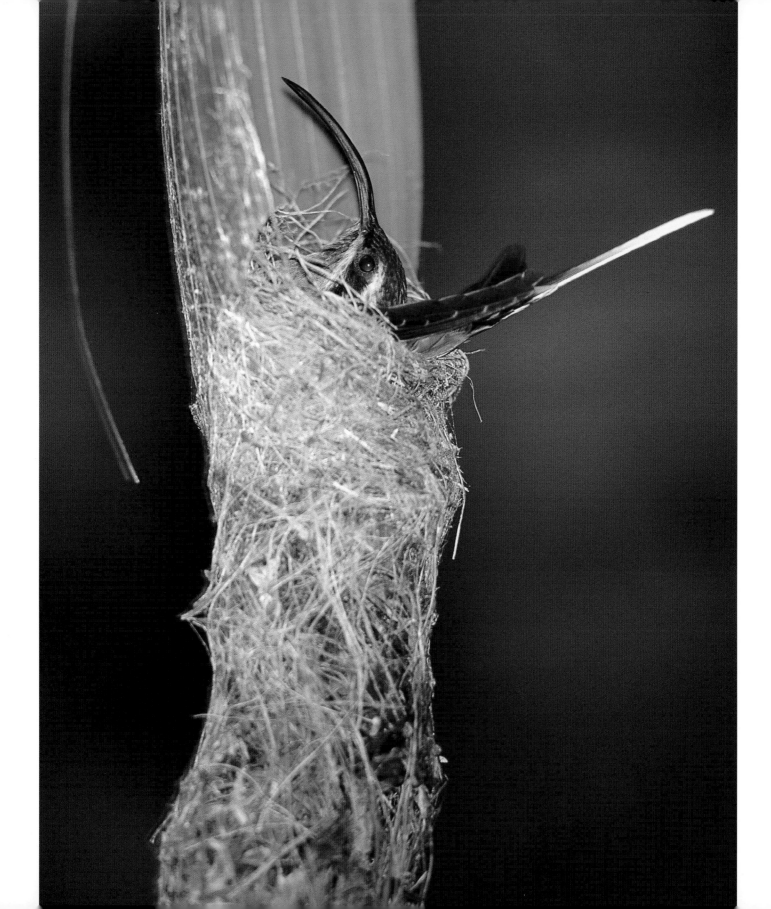

terrestrial predators. As a rule, hummingbird nests are sheltered above by leaves or branches, which provide a defense against flying predators as well as an umbrella against rain and a shield against heat loss. Hummingbirds often show fidelity to their nesting site, returning year after year and, on occasion, rebuilding their old nest, or sometimes building a new nest on the ruins of the old one, making a condo-like structure.

Almost invariably hummingbirds lay two eggs, usually forty-eight hours apart. The eggs are exceedingly small, each the size of a pinto bean or raisin. Even so, together they represent up to a third of the hummingbird's weight, and relatively speaking, they drain a good deal more energy from the female than the larger eggs of other species, demonstrating yet again the extraordinary energetic demands that attend all hummingbird activity.

The eggs also take a relatively long period to incubate, on average a minimum of fifteen to seventeen days. The reason for this extended incubation period is that the female must leave the nest frequently to replenish her own energy supply, thus prolonging the incubation period. Even so, eggs are covered 60 to 80 percent of the time under normal circumstances. Usually, incubating females do not enter torpor, as the lowering of their body temperature would further prolong the incubation period. However, William Calder observed two broad-tailed hummingbirds on their nesting grounds in the Rockies that were forced to remain on their nests because of rainy conditions, causing them to miss a significant portion of their feeding time. Both responded by entering torpor, even though they were incubating and egg temperatures might drop. The longer incubation period of hummingbirds nesting high in the Andes might well relate to their frequent need to resort to nighttime torpor. The Andean hillstar, for example, has the longest incubation period of any hummingbird, up to twenty-three days.

The insulating quality of the nest is important in maintaining the heat balance

*Hermit hummingbirds, such as this long-tailed hermit in Costa Rica, often build their elongated nests on the underside of palm leaves as protection against rain and predators.* KEVIN SCHAFER

THE INSULATING

QUALITY OF THE NEST

IS IMPORTANT IN

MAINTAINING THE HEAT

BALANCE OF BOTH

THE FEMALE AND THE

EGGS.

of both the female and the eggs. North American mountain species, such as the calliope and broad-tailed hummingbirds, choose nests sites that are sheltered by spruce boughs or overhung by a canopy if they are nesting in aspen. In either case, the branches shield the nest from the heat sink of the cold night sky and provide protection from the wind—cutting heat loss by half. Such protection is of even greater significance to the nestlings.

When the hatchlings do arrive, they are, to quote Skutch, "ugly, unpromising little grubs." They are blind, naked (possessing no downy coat), and helpless. Like all newborns they have a seemingly insatiable capacity and need for food. The mother feeds her nestlings one to three times an hour. She regurgitates nectar and insects from her own crop and then uses her needlelike bill to inject food into the hungry, gape-mouthed young. As their crops are crammed full, they become grotesquely distended, giving the impression that the nestlings suffer from a goiter condition.

The mother will often cover the nestlings with her body—brooding them—when it rains, or stand on the nest edge shading them from hot sun. Generally speaking, by twelve days of age, the chicks have attained the ability to control their own body temperature, even though they are still mostly naked.

By sixteen days, the nestlings have grown feathers. At this stage they begin to exercise their wings while holding onto the nest edge for dear life. After several days of wing exercise, they take their first experimental flight to a nearby perch. They are also learning how to feed at this time and will dart out their tongue at insects passing within reach. They fledge fully at twenty-one to twenty-five days and fly well from the very beginning. Although they now begin to forage and feed themselves, their mother often continues to feed them for at least another two weeks.

Female hummingbirds have been described as "the most tenacious and persistent of mothers." They are as aggressive in their defense of the nesting site

FACING PAGE

*These newly hatched Anna's hummingbirds conform to the description "ugly, unpromising little grubs." Successful fledging of young is discouragingly low, averaging 20 to 50 percent for different species.*

RICHARD R. HANSEN

as the pugnacious males are in their patrol of feeding and breeding territories. They attack any and all interlopers, even humans and hawks.

Sometimes discretion is the better part of valor in the hummingbird's defense of the young. In a study carried out by Wildlife Rescue of New Mexico, it was observed that black-chinned hummingbird mothers and nestlings were uncharacteristically quiet during feeding at the nest. This behavior, common among hummingbirds, is in sharp contrast to that of many other bird species, in which nestlings use loud vocalizations to induce feeding—the louder the hungry nestlings are, the more they appear to get fed. Because black-chinned hummingbirds are notorious for building their nests in exposed locations, easily seen and reached by predators, especially avian ones, they must be quiet to avoid drawing undue attention to the nest. After fledging, when the young birds are less vulnerable to predation, they do call when they are hungry or distressed.

Most female birds will continue to brood infertile eggs long after their expected date of hatching, and they will even attend dead chicks. Only the most dire circumstances can lead to the breakdown of this parental bond. In rare circumstances, mothers prematurely abandon the eggs or leave live chicks unattended. Calder observed this behavior in broad-tails when they were forced to spend more and more time away from the nest because of a sudden decline in their food supply, in concert with an influx of migratory rufous hummingbirds which aggressively claimed feeding territories. It became a case of energetic triage for the brooding females, who could not meet their energetic needs and those of the chicks as well— and so, in the end, abandoned the nest.

Infertility, abandonment, accidents, and extreme weather can all contribute to an untimely end for chicks. But predation is by far the most important factor in their mortality. A study carried out in the American southwest showed that predation accounted for nearly 80 percent of all failures to fledge young. Predation on eggs accounted for 70 percent of the losses, while the balance was due to attacks on nestlings. Mexican jays, hooded orioles, and summer tanagers were three of the avian culprits identified. Snakes were thought to be responsible for the losses to broad-billed hummingbird nests, since these nests were often located close to the ground. Overall, broad-bills fared well, successfully fledging young 80 percent of the time. Generally speaking, for all hummingbirds successful hatching and fledging of young is discouragingly low, ranging between 20 and 50 percent. In a year when catastrophic weather conditions prevail, no chicks may survive.

## DEATH BY A THOUSAND MEANS

If they survive the vulnerable nesting phase, hummingbirds appear to suffer relatively low mortality rates as adults. Even so, their predators are legion: larger birds, amphibians, even insects. The literature on hummingbird loss is a litany of untimely and unlikely ends. Among the notable winged predators of hummingbirds are orioles, flycatchers, small hawks, falcons, and even roadrunners.

Bruce Wright, former director of the Northwestern Wildlife Station in Fredericton, New Brunswick, recounted a fatal attack on a hummingbird by a Baltimore oriole:

> My wife and I were watching a male Baltimore oriole on a shrub in our garden on 4 June 1961. Two male orioles had been feeding on blossoms without apparent friction, while two pairs of Ruby-throated hummingbirds also worked over the flowers. A male hummingbird hovered in front of a blossom within about one-third meter of one of the male orioles. The oriole turned, pounced, and caught the hummingbird in its beak. It then flew to a nearby branch and held the hummingbird down with its feet and pecked at it violently until feathers flew from it. When I approached to observe more closely, the oriole flew and dropped the hummingbird to the ground. When I picked the little bird up, it was dead.

FACING PAGE

*An eyelash viper strikes at a rufous-tailed hummingbird, narrowly missing it.*

MICHAEL & PATRICIA FOGDEN

A brown-crested flycatcher near Portal, Arizona, deliberately collided with a rufous hummingbird in midair, then plucked the stunned bird from the ground by grasping a wing in its beak. The flycatcher flew to a nearby perch and proceeded to dispatch the smaller bird by knocking it against the branch with violent side-to-side motions of its head. In a second incident near Portal, a roadrunner stalked a black-chinned hummingbird from a porch roof under which a hummingbird feeder was hung.

Danger not only comes from above but lurks below. On several occasions, frogs, in particular leopard frogs, have been observed dispatching hummingbirds. In one recorded instance in 1939, in Gimli, Manitoba, a frog snapped up a hummingbird while it was feeding at a flower border, and the bird's body was later recovered from the dissected amphibian. It is possible that the frogs mistake the low-flying hummingbirds for large insects. Not surprisingly, reptiles—both lizards and snakes—also prey upon hummingbirds, young and old.

Even given the diminutive size of hummingbirds, it is surprising that insects have, on occasion, effectively preyed upon them. There are a number of documented cases of preying mantises capturing a hummingbird and in one case actually killing it. The latter instance was recorded by Christella Butler of Philadelphia:

> Late in the afternoon of September 17, 1948, I saw a mantis poised on an orange-colored zinnia. When a hummingbird [ruby-throated] flew to the flower, the mantis seized the bird. I hastened to rescue the bird, but even after both had been removed to the ground the mantis would not release its hold. As the two were forcibly separated, bits of feathers held by the mantis were torn from the bird. The only blood to appear was from the bill of the bird.

Hummingbirds have become entangled in spiders' webs and caught on the hooked spines of burdock and even impaled on cactus spines. Despite these almost constant depredations and accidents, hummingbirds as a species are surprisingly long lived, especially in light of their size and high-energy lifestyle. The average female life expectancy is 2.8 years, compared with 2.05 for males, with the greatest mortality occurring in the first two years of life. Individuals may live much longer, however, and the maximum hummingbird life span is double the expected maximum life span for a wild bird of that size. One banded ruby-throated hummingbird was recaptured after 9 years, and a broad-tailed hummingbird is known to have lived at least 12.1 years. The latter, interestingly, had two gray feathers on her crown.

Hummingbirds share with humans the ability to live longer than their size would suggest they should. Another parallel between humans and hummingbirds is the fact that on average females in both populations live longer than males.

The fundamental reason for the longevity of hummingbirds has not been adequately explained. Whatever the reason, the ability of females to live longer is especially important to the survival of the species because it allows for more breeding seasons.

Hummingbirds incubate only two eggs, probably because without the help of the male, the female cannot provide for more young. The hummingbirds in the temperate climes of North America are further constrained by the short flowering season, especially at high latitudes and altitudes, to having only one clutch per season. One southwestern species, the blue-throated hummingbird, usually raises two broods in a season—and most species will try for a second clutch if their first clutch or chicks are lost. Since only one of the two chicks usually fledges, it is necessary for the hummingbird to live long enough to have sufficient breeding seasons to replace herself and her breeding partner in the population.

PAGES 92–93

*The white-necked jacobin is*

*often associated with lowland*

*forests such as this one in*

*Trinidad. Male birds are*

*usually solitary but may form*

*leklike groups to attract*

*females.* ROGER ERIKSSON

The female improves her chances of doing so not only by living longer but also by carefully choosing her nest site close to a food source, by building a thickly insulated and well-concealed nest, and by tenaciously attending to her eggs and chicks. In addition, despite the horror stories of being gulped by frogs and snakes and snagged by winged predators, large and small, from hawks to preying mantises, hummingbirds enjoy a relatively low vulnerability to both disease and predation. In short, they are diminutive models of Darwinian fitness.

## HUMMERS AND HUMANS: AN EVOLVING RELATIONSHIP

In the past, hummingbirds were exploited for their beautiful feathers. During the Victorian era, hummingbird feathers and whole birds were used extensively as adornments for garments, especially hats. In 1888, more than 400,000 hummingbird skins were auctioned in London. Some of the tropical species sacrificed for fashion have never been seen again. As late as the first decade of the twentieth century, some 150,000 North American hummingbirds were shipped overseas.

In the more recent past, we can take heart in the knowledge that the proliferation of feeders seems to be helping to maintain healthy hummingbird populations and, in some instances, to expand some species' traditional ranges. This success, if we can call it that, is due to a happy circumstance that the cane or beet sugar we use in feeders is the same sugar (sucrose) preferred by hummingbirds in their natural food source, nectar.

Hummingbirds are expanding both their breeding and wintering ranges eastward and northward, in response to the introduction of feeders as well as to the cultivation of urban and suburban exotic plants. Anna's hummingbird, for example, has dramatically expanded its breeding range. Before the 1930s, it bred only from northern Baja California north to San Francisco Bay. It now breeds north to Vancouver Island, British Columbia, and eastward to southern Arizona, and is known to have nested at least once in Texas. The introduction of tree tobacco and eucalyptus, which bloom when other flowers do not, seems to be the reason that hummingbirds linger in breeding areas in southern California chaparral habitat through the summer and fall rather than migrating, by necessity, to montane meadows. In addition, the Anna's hummingbird's penchant for gardens has given it a reputation as an urban hummingbird.

Feeders and gardens have also enticed an increasing variety and number of hummingbirds to alter their wintering pattern. Winter vagrants have been showing up with some regularity in the southeastern United States in recent years. Not so long ago, it was believed that the ruby-throated hummingbird was the only hummingbird commonly found east of the Mississippi, considered a barrier across which western hummers would not trespass. However, one of the westernmost hummers, the rufous, has long since transgressed this supposed boundary. The first eastern record dates from 1909, but the specimen lay in the South Carolina Museum in Charleston for nineteen years, misidentified as a ruby-throat. Since mid-century, rufous hummingbirds have been sighted up and down the Eastern Seaboard, from as far north as Nova Scotia south to Florida. This pattern probably relates to the elliptical migration route of the rufous, which describes an almost perfectly oval path: in spring it follows a northwestward route along coastal Mexico and the United States, but in midsummer it returns on a southeastward route along the tops of the eastern ridges of the Rockies. Some of these southward migrants obviously drift far to the east, where they are now found to be overwintering in Mississippi, Alabama, and Louisiana.

The Hummer/Bird Study Group centered in Clay, Alabama, has banded eleven overwintering species in the southeastern United States. The old gardens of south

PAGE 96

*Berylline hummingbirds are widespread in the wooded highlands of Mexico and Central America. Because they rarely breed north of Mexico, nearly all of the U.S. records of these birds are from southeastern Arizona.* BARRETT & MACKAY PHOTO

PAGE 97

*A green-crowned brilliant at a feeder in Monteverde, Costa Rica, displays all the brilliance of its name. Feeders seem to help maintain healthy hummingbird populations.* S. J. KRASEMANN/PETER ARNOLD, INC.

Louisiana sporadically host broad-billed, buff-bellied, black-chinned, Anna's, rufous, Allen's, calliope, and broad-tailed hummers. Rarities, such as magnificent, white-eared, and a single green violet-ear, have also shown up in the southeast in recent years.

The proliferation of feeders in recent decades seems primarily responsible for the marked changes in hummingbird distribution. Feeders provide a supplemental food supply when flowers are not in bloom, especially early and late in the breeding season and after weather or disease damages or wipes out natural flower patches. In mitigating the effects of these natural fluctuations in the natural food supply, feeders are helping to boost some populations above natural levels.

Biologists view these apparently positive effects of feeders with caution, however. While supplementing or replacing natural food sources, feeders often expose hummingbirds to unnatural predation, disease, or other sources of mortality. Feeders located near windows result in fatal collisions; domestic cats also stalk hummers using feeders. Failure to regularly replace sugar solutions in feeders can result in the growth of noxious molds. Sugar solutions also attract hornets, which have been known to knock down hummingbirds in midair—apparently by stinging them—and to prey upon nestlings.

Concern has been expressed that maintaining feeders late in the season can cause hummingbirds to delay their migration and that this delay can make them vulnerable to cold weather. Although individual migratory hummingbirds may linger north of their normal wintering areas, at their peril, the vast majority of the population does migrate on time. Feeders can do little to override such migratory instincts, honed by millions of years of natural selection, and in fact may be beneficial to those few individuals whose instincts do misfire. "There is overwhelming evidence that normal, healthy hummingbirds migrate in response to cues such as changing day length, not cold weather or lack of food," says biologist

Sheri Williamson of the Southeastern Arizona Bird Observatory. "The few birds that migrate behind schedule are often young or physically challenged, and feeders can give these birds a second chance at survival."

The case of a broad-tailed hummingbird that overwintered in Tucson, in two successive years, rather than migrating south to Mexico, may be a harbinger of future trends. Since this species normally winters in the mountains of the state of Jalisco in Mexico, food supply rather than temperature probably limits its northern distribution in winter. Artificial watering of the dry Sonoran landscape and the use of feeders, however, allowed it to survive north of its traditional winter range. Such pioneering events may have been what allowed hummingbirds to expand northward from the tropics in the first place. Over time, global warming may create conditions for further expansion of tropical species northward.

Human alteration of the natural habitat is a matter of concern with some hummingbird species. In *The Birds of Arizona,* Costa's hummingbird is described as "the dry desert hummingbird par excellence," with the Sonoran desert scrub being the heart of its range. Although this desert habitat, covering northern Mexico and the extreme southwest of the U.S., remains largely intact, alterations are accelerating. Residential expansion in Arizona and California is removing many of the natural desert plants exploited for food and nesting sites by the Costa's hummingbird. In California the bird's preferred breeding habitat of coastal scrub has all but been eliminated. The most serious threat is the clearing of desert scrub, thorn forest, and montane forest, primarily in Sonora, Mexico, and to a lesser degree in southwestern Arizona, in order to plant South African buffelgrass as cattle forage. This drought-resistant grass is fire-prone, and by fueling repeated fires can eliminate paloverdes and other nest trees.

Other endemic hummers, such as Anna's hummingbirds, have readily switched to feeders and exotic plants as food sources, but because of their much larger size they tend to outcompete Costa's hummingbirds. In addition, the latter appear to

Hummingbirds are expanding both

their breeding and wintering ranges

eastward and northward, in

response to the

introduction of

feeders as well as

to the cultivation of

urban and suburban

exotic plants.

show a predilection for wild areas, avoiding urban centers such as Tucson and Phoenix, at least during the breeding season.

The loss of natural habitat along the migratory corridor in south Texas, between Corpus Christi and Brownsville, could affect ruby-throats. Much of this area has been converted to agriculture, with a loss of nectar-producing plants essential to fuel migration.

As with many other Neotropical migrants, there is also concern about destruction of forest habitat on wintering grounds in southern Mexico and Central America. The impact on hummingbirds, if there is a significant one, has not been well studied, however. In recent decades, more buff-bellied hummingbirds, which occupy a coastal band from the Yucatán to western Florida, have been observed in the United States, prompting suggestions that the loss of forest habitat to agriculture in eastern and northeastern Mexico has forced more of them northward—but again, there are few data to substantiate such an assertion.

A different, and paradoxical, picture emerges in the United States and Canada. Here, clear-cutting may encourage the growth of hummingbird flowers, temporarily increasing their abundance. The calliope hummingbird, for example, seems to select early shrub stages after clear-cutting for breeding territory, indicating a benefit to the species, at least in the short term. Forest management practices often preclude natural succession, however. A study of the use of silvicultural herbicides in Nova Scotia found no ruby-throated hummingbirds in plots where the natural succession of hardwoods after clear-cutting had been suppressed by herbicides. To date, very little specific information exists about the direct effects of such synthetic chemicals on any species of hummingbirds.

Ironically—considering the concentration of North American media on deforestation in the tropics—clear-cutting in western Canada and the United States

FACING PAGE

*Calliope hummingbirds seem to select early shrub stages after clear-cutting for breeding territory. Boosting migrant populations, however, may ultimately have a negative effect on species native to Mexico and Central America, where many migrants overwinter.* WAYNE & HELEN LANKINEN

may have long-distance effects on hummingbirds native to the wintering grounds. If migrant populations are boosted by clear-cutting here, as well as by the use of feeders, they might well "swamp Mexican endemics, ultimately contributing to the decline of the latter," according to William Calder. At the same time, the suppression of natural fires, which create good conditions for hummingbirds, may nullify any such long-distance effects of clear-cutting.

Further research is needed to address this and other conservation concerns related to hummingbirds over their entire range. If we have learned anything, it should be that simple abundance in the present is no guarantee for the future of a species. Also, we always must be mindful of the fact that human intervention into the workings of nature, even when well-intentioned, can have undesirable results.

For now, overall, North American hummingbird populations seem to be thriving and as such are a rare wildlife success story to counter our litany of losses. Interestingly, our small success in this instance is due not to any concerted effort as a society to save species but is the consequence of our cumulative individual desire to have these beautiful birds as part of our surroundings, underscoring how personal action can have a positive impact on the environment.

*Broad-tailed hummingbird*
*chicks test their wings. The use*
*of feeders may allow*
*this species to expand its*
*winter range northward.*
JEFF FOOTT/BBC NATURAL
HISTORY UNIT

# FOR FURTHER READING

Audubon, John James. 1957. "Ruby-Throated Hummingbird." In *The Bird Biographies of John James Audubon*. Edited by A. Ford. New York: MacMillan.

Baltosser, W. H., and P. E. Scott. 1996. *Costa's Hummingbird*. The Birds of North America, no. 251. Philadelphia: The Academy of Natural Sciences.

Bent, A. C. 1964. *Life Histories of North American Cuckoos, Goatsuckers, Hummingbirds and Their Allies*. New York: Dover Publications.

Calder, W. A. 1993. *Rufous Hummingbird*. The Birds of North America, no. 53. Philadelphia: The Academy of Natural Sciences.

Calder, W. A., and L. L. Calder. 1992. *Broad-Tailed Hummingbird*. The Birds of North America, no. 16. Philadelphia: The Academy of Natural Sciences.

Calder, W. A., and L. L. Calder. 1994. *Calliope Hummingbird*. The Birds of North America, no. 134. Philadelphia: The Academy of Natural Sciences.

DesGranges, Jean-Luc, and P. R. Grant. 1990. "Migrant Hummingbirds' Accommodation into Tropical Communities." In *Migrant Birds in the Neotropics: Ecology, Behavior, Distribution, and Conservation*. Edited by A. Keast and E. S. Morton. Washington, D. C.: Smithsonian Institution Press.

Grant, K. A., and V. Grant. 1968. *Hummingbirds and Their Flowers*. New York: Columbia University Press.

Greenewalt, C. II. 1990. *Hummingbirds*. New York: Dover Publications.

Johnsgard, P. A. 1997. *The Hummingbirds of North America*. 2d ed. Washington, D. C.: Smithsonian Institution Press.

Lazaroff, D. W. 1995. *The Secret Lives of Hummingbirds*. Tucson: Arizona-Sonora Desert Museum Press.

Long, K. 1997. *Hummingbirds, A Wildlife Handbook*. Boulder, Colo.: Johnson Books.

Powers, D. R. 1996. *Magnificent Hummingbird*. The Birds of North America, no. 221. Philadelphia: The Academy of Natural Sciences.

Robinson, T. R., R. R. Sargeant, and M. B. Sargeant. 1996. *Ruby-Throated Hummingbird*. The Birds of North America, no. 204. Philadelphia: The Academy of Natural Sciences.

Russell, S. M. 1996. *Anna's Hummingbird*. The Birds of North America, no. 226. Philadelphia: The Academy of Natural Sciences.

Scott, P. E. 1994. *Lucifer Hummingbird*. The Birds of North America, no. 134. Philadelphia: The Academy of Natural Sciences.

Skutch, A. F. 1973. *The Life of the Hummingbird*. New York: Crown Publishers.

True, D. 1994. *Hummingbirds of North America: Attracting, Feeding, and Photographing*. Albuquerque: University of New Mexico Press.

Tyrrell, E. Q., and R. A. Tyrrell. 1985. *Hummingbirds, Their Life and Behavior: A Photographic Study of the North American Species*. New York: Crown Publishers.

# INDEX